RAYMOND ROUSSEL at nineteen
at the time he was writing *La Doublure*

(Photographed in Milan, October 1896)

In his will Roussel requested this photograph be used as the frontispiece for all his posthumous works.

RAYMOND ROUSSEL:
LIFE, DEATH & WORKS
Essays and Stories by Various Hands

Being a Special Issue of
ATLAS ANTHOLOGY

(No. 4)

ATLAS PRESS,
Publishers, London, 1987

Raymond Roussel: Life, Death & Works is published by
Atlas Press, 10 Park st, London SE1

© 1987, Atlas Press
All Rights Reserved
© for translations remains with the translator

ISBN 0-947757-14-7

Permission to use the following texts has been given by:
Jean-Michel Place for Dali's "Nouvelles Impressions d'Afrique" from
"Le Surrealisme au Service de la Revolution".
Editions J.J.Pauvert for Breton's "Raymond Roussel" from
"Anthologie de l'humour noir", © 1966, 1972, Jean-Jacques Pauvert, 1979,
Societe Nouvelle des Editions Pauvert.
Editions Gallimard for Ferry's letters and
"Raymond Roussel au Paradis" from "Le Mecanicien et autres contes" © 1953.
Michel Leiris and Editions Fata Morgana for Leiris' "Conception et Realite chez
Raymond Roussel".
L'Arc for John Ashbery's "Introduction" and Raymond Roussel's "A la Havane".
John Calder for Robbe-Grillet's "Enigme et transparence chez Raymond Roussel".

Sellerio editore for Sciascia's "Atti relativi alla morte di Raymond Roussel", © 1979.
Mme. Guerin-Grondin for Vitrac's "Raymond Roussel".
Editions de Minuit for Butor's "Sur les procedes de Raymond Roussel © 1960
Editions L'Herne for Ricardou's "Disparition elocutoire" © 1972
Photographs reproduced with the permission of John Ashbery and Francois Caradec.

This book designed by: Alastair Brotchie.

Printed by SRP ltd., Exeter, England.

British Library Cataloguing in Publication Data:
Raymond Roussel: life, death & works.—
(Atlas anthology; 4)
1. Roussel, raymond — Criticism and interpretation
848'.91209   PQ2635.096168Z/
ISBN 0-947757-14-7 pbk

Contents

Editors' Prefaces *8*

Roussel Chronology. *11*

ANDREW THOMSON & VARIOUS CRITICS

Mots relatifs aux actes de Raymond Roussel—*Selections from the Critical Writings about Roussel's Theatre* *13*

ROBERT DE MONTESQUIOU

A Difficult Author. *25*

PHILIPPE SOUPAULT

Raymond Roussel *34*

PIERRE JANET

The Psychological Characteristics of Ecstasy. *38*

ROGER VITRAC

Raymond Roussel *43*

SALVADOR DALI

Raymond Roussel:Nouvelles Impressions d'Afrique. *55*

ANDRÉ BRETON

Raymond Roussel *57*

MICHEL BUTOR

The Methods of Raymond Roussel *60*

JEAN FERRY

Raymond Roussel in Paradise *72*

Two Letters to Jacques Brunius. *106*

MICHEL LEIRIS

Conception and Reality in the Work of Raymond Roussel. *73*

JOHN ASHBERY

Introduction to Raymond Roussel's "In Havana" *86*

RAYMOND ROUSSEL

In Havana *92*

An Unpublished Note. *98*

ALAIN ROBBE-GRILLET

Riddles and Transparencies in Raymond Roussel. *100*

JEAN RICARDOU

Elocutory Disappearance *111*

LEONARDO SCIASCIA

Acts Relative to the Death of Raymond Roussel *124*

APPENDICES

I. M. Raymond Roussel's House on Wheels by F.T. *149*

II. Raymond Roussel in English, bibliography. *153*

Autumn   1987

Editors: Alastair Brotchie
         Malcolm Green
         Antony Melville

Associate editor for this issue:
         Andrew Thomson

We would like to thank the following for their generous assistance: Mme. Arlette Albert-Birot, John Ashbery, Francois Caradec, Thieri Foulc, Mme. Laura Fronty, Paul Gayot, Mme. Guerin-Grondin, Michel Leiris, John Lyle, Jean-Michel Place, Philippe Soupault, Trevor Winkfield, and all our long-suffering translators.

Atlas Anthology is published by Atlas Press, 10 Park st., Borough, London SE1 9AB, Tel: (01) 378-7861.

We *EXHORT* our readers to write to be put on our mailing list, as we are planning some future publications which will only be available directly from us.

The essays and texts in this collection constitute a virtual history of Roussel criticism and exegesis, and they are printed here in chronological order, so far as that is possible. Most are translated for the first time. However, several are not–this and the differing interpretations of translators means that certain passages recur throughout the book in different versions. We have not attempted to harmonise them. The bibliography at the end includes the contents of the present volume and provides full details of first publication etc. Notes and editorial comment are credited in square brackets–all uncredited notes (except this one!) are by . . . . [Alastair Brotchie]

*

[Andrew Thomson] *writes: The majority of the texts in this article were originally printed in newspapers or theatrical magazines (such as the daily review* Comoedia*) which are housed in the Bibliotheque de l'Arsenal, Fonds Rondel. An exception to this is the excerpt from Youki Desnos' book* Les Confidences de Youki, *published in 1957 by Fayard, Paris. It is worth noting that Edouard Dujardin, author of the piece on page 18 was also the author of* Les Lauriers sont coupés, *the novel which Joyce acknowledged as the prototype of the* monologue interieur, *and hence the source of inspiration for Molly Bloom's soliloquy. (An English version was published by the Mandrake Press with a preface by George Moore.)*

My selections and translations have been made from the texts as they appear in Francois Caradec's Vie de Raymond Roussel *(Pauvert, Paris, 1972) and* Bizarre, 34/35, *ed. Jean Ferry (Pauvert, 1964).*

Robert de Montesquiou-Fezensac *(1855-1921) achieved a vicarious and unwanted fame as the original of Proust's "Baron de Charlus", Huysman's "Des Esseintes" and Lorrain's "Monsieur de Phocas". The arbiter of fashionable "decadent" taste in his day, he was like Proust and Roussel, a rich homosexual aristocrat. He corresponded with Roussel on literary matters– they exchanged books–and Roussel makes several appearances in his novels.*

The study printed here is the first half of his essay "A Difficult Author", the second half is devoted to La Vue. *The two sections were written at different times, the section on* Impressions d'Afrique *is a revision of an article Montesquiou wrote for the periodical* Gil Blas *in 1914.*

Philippe Soupault *(born 1897). When Soupault wrote this piece for the proto-Surrealist review* Littérature, *he had met Roussel on two occasions, on the first he declined to discuss anything except music, on the second, Jules Verne.*

Pierre Janet *(1859-1947) Professor of Psychiatric Medicine, one of Jung's teachers, author of numerous standard works, Janet appears never to have realised that Roussel was not just another wealthy neurasthenic.*

Roger Vitrac *(1899-1951), a playwright connected for a period to the surrealists, wrote this article, the first of any substance, for* **La Nouvelle Revue Francaise,** *Feb, 1928. It is a mark of the contemporary interest in Roussel, no doubt due to the scandal of* **Locus Solus,** *that it was published in English only a month later.*

Salvador Dali *(born 1904). This review was published in* **Le Surréalisme au Service de la Revolution,** *VI, 1933.*

Andre Breton *(1896-1966). Breton wrote several essays on Roussel, this was intended to preface a selection of Roussel's works in Breton's* **Anthologie de l'humour noir,** *however the first edition was unaccompanied by these works— by this time Roussel's family was attempting to live down its infamous son, and permission to publish them was witheld.*

Michel Butor *(born 1926) Novelist and essayist. This text was reprinted in the first volume of his collected essays* **Repertoire.**

Jean Ferry *(1906-1974) No book on Roussel would be complete without something by his chief hagiographer Jean Ferry, the "Régent par susception transseante de doxodoxie Rousselliennes" of the the Collège de Pataphysique. Ferry wrote two impressive and entertaining works on Roussel:* **Une étude sur Raymond Roussel,** *Arcanes, Paris, 1953, and* **L'Afrique des Impressions,** *College de Pataphysique & Pauvert, 1967, and also edited his complete works for Pauvert.*
These letters to the cineast Jacques Brunius, which have not been published before, concern his "Etude" and its introduction. The story is from **Le Mécanicien et autres contes,** *originally published in 1950, and then by Gallimard in 1953.*

Michel Leiris *(born 1901) Ethnologist, autobiographer, novelist, pataphysician, surrealist etc, Leiris was related to Roussel—but for this fortunate coincidence biographical information would be almost non-existent.*

John Ashbery *(born 1927) Poet and art critic, John Ashbery did a lot of research into the life and work of Roussel in the late '50's—in the process he discovered most of the extant photographs as well as the ms. he introduces here. The letter from Roussel which he has kindly lent us is printed here more as a sample of the master's hand than for its literary interest!*

Alain Robbe-Grillet *Novelist and theorist of the* **nouveau roman,** *his early works were directly inspired by the poetry of Roussel. This essay, ostensibly a review of Foucault's book about Roussel, did much to revive interest in Roussel's work.*

Jean Ricardou. *Novelist associated with the* **nouveau roman,** *this text was written as an introduction to the French edition of Sciascia's essay.*

Leonardo Sciascia *(born 1921) Sicilian author of distinguished political thrillers and detective novels. His most recent work concerns the assassination of Aldo Moro.*

F.T. *An unknown hack for* **La Revue du Touring Club de France,** *who originally published this execrably written description of Roussel's "roulotte" in 1926.*

Raymond Roussel's place of birth.

Most of Roussel's works first appeared in the popular newspaper Le Gaulois
de Dimanche *before their book publication, only some of these appearances
are noted here, all his books were published by the firm of Alphonse Lemerre.*

1877   Birth of Raymond Roussel on the 20th. of January at his parents'
        house No 25, Boulevard Malesherbes, Paris. He has an elder brother
        and sister.

1883   The Roussel family move to No 50, rue de Chaillot, near the
        Champs-Elysees.

1891   After one failure he is admitted to the Paris Conservatoire as a piano
        student.

1894   "I decided to abandon music altogether to devote myself entirely
        to verse . . ." He writes *Mon Ame*, and, in fact, he only abandons
        composition, but continues his piano studies.

1895   Continues to achieve excellent results at the examinations at the
        Conservatoire.

1896   Writes *La Doublure* and undergoes the "crisis" described by Dr.
        Janet whose patient he soon becomes. While in Milan with his mother,
        his favourite portrait is taken (see frontispiece).

1897   Once again he passes his examinations easily. First publications:
        La Doublure (Lemerre) and later *Mon Ame* (Le Gaulois...). Meets
        Proust, a close neighbour.

1898   Military service at Amiens (until 1901), and a single meeting with
        his hero, "that man of incommensurable genius", Jules Verne.

1900   *Chiquenaude*, the first published work to employ "the method",
        appears (Lemerre).

1901   Death of elder brother.

1902   After his sister's marriage, Roussel and his mother now live alone.

1903   *La Vue, Le Concert* (in Le Gaulois...).

1904   *La Vue* in book form (Lemerre). An utter commercial failure, this
        edition was not exhausted until 1953.

1907   The first prose works begin to appear in Le Gaulois.., *Nanon*, and
        then:

1908   *Une Page de Folklore Breton.*

1910   *Impressions d'Afrique* (Lemerre). Meets Charlotte Dufrène, his
        "mistress of convenience".

1911   Theatrical performances of *Impressions d'Afrique*. Death of his
        mother in Biarritz, he inherits a large fortune.

1912   *Impressions d'Afrique* revived at the Theatre Antoine, it is greeted with astonishment and ridicule.

1914   *Locus Solus* (Lemerre). Makes the acquaintance of Robert de Montesquiou, an early admirer of his work. Rejoins army.

1915   Begins work on *Nouvelles Impressions d'Afrique.*

1918   *Pages Choises* (Lemerre)—selections from *Impressions d'Afrique* and *Locus Solus.* Meets Cocteau.

1920   Travels in India, Australia, New Zealand, the Pacific Archipelagi, China, Japan and America.

1922   Theatrical adaptation of *Locus Solus* at the Theatre Antoine, another scandal.

1924   Theatrical performances of *L'Étoile au Front.* Roussel's travels in his "roulotte", a luxuriously appointed travelling home, begin at about this time (the roulotte was exhibited at the Salon de L'Auto in 1925).

1925   Publication of *L'Étoile au Front* (Lemerre), meeting with Vitrac.

1926   Performance of *La Poussière de Soleils.* Travels in the roulotte to Italy and Austria.

1927   Publication of *La Poussière de Soleils* (Lemerre) and its revival at the Theatre de la Renaissance. Travels in Greece, Asia Minor, Persia, and re-visits Egypt.

1928   First disintoxication cure at a sanatorium where he meets Cocteau again.

1931   Increased use of barbiturates, probably writes *Comment j'ai écrit certains de mes livres* at this time.

1932   *Nouvelles Impressions d'Afrique* (Lemerre). Applies himself to chess, Tartakower publishes articles on his formula for the knight/bishop checkmate.

1933   In January he makes his will and arranges for the posthumous publication of *Comment j'ai écrit certains de mes livres.* Travels to Sicily and reaches Palermo on the 3rd or 4th of June. He dies on the night of the 13th or morning of the 14th of July. He is buried in Père-Lachaise cemetery on the 26th July.

1935   Publication of *Comment j'ai écrit certains de mes livres* (Lemerre).

1963   Editions J.-J. Pauvert begin re-publication of Roussel's complete works.

ANDREW THOMSON & VARIOUS CRITICS
Mots relatifs aux Actes de Raymond Roussel – Selections from the critical writings about Roussel's theatre

Translations   Andrew Thomson

Roussel's experience with the theatre seems to have followed a broadly similar path to his development as a writer, namely an experience of "success" (or ecstacy), followed by a series of unsuccessful attempts to recapture that initial glory:

"The only kind of success I have ever really experienced derived from singing to my own piano accompaniment and above all my numerous impersonations of actors and ordinary folk. But there at least my success was enormous."[1]

It was presumably for such success that Roussel yearned as he sat watching the failure of his four big theatrical ventures. Failure, that is, on his terms. Michel Leiris recalled the kind of theatre Roussel "adored":

". . . dramas by Victorien Sardou (and historical plays in general), melo-dramas (notably *La Bouquetière des Innocents*—which he went to see twelve or fifteen times in succession, and *La Tour de Nesle*), the Trianon Lyrique operettas, the plays of Georges Feydeau, vaudeville with racy dialogue. He had a horror of psychological plays, of theatre of 'ideas'; particularily that of Henry Bataille, which he described as 'turgid'."[2]

Roussel's adaptation of *Impressions d'Afrique* opened at the Théâtre Femina on September 30th 1911, but was suspended after a week because of the death of his mother. These performances passed virtually unnoticed in the press. The play re-opened at the Théâtre Antoine on 11th May 1912 and ran until June 5th 1912:[3]

The public looked on in sceptical or even rebellious mood. Three spectators of the common sort, who were sitting behind me, displayed noisy ill-will. They were doing what all discontented Frenchmen do: resolutely hurling witticisms. God preserve you, readers, from being thus caught between two fires.
—Henry Bidou, **Journal des débats**, 20th May, 1912

Scenes from Impressions d'Afrique: *the zither played by an earthworm, the voluntary execution of Djizme by lightning, and the shipwrecked passengers encounter King Talou.*

I have heard the laughs which this play aroused before, when **Ubu Roi** was performed. Nowadays **Ubu** is frequently said to be a masterpiece. In several years

. . . No more will we see the black monarch Talou, the scientist with the umbrella and the folding stool, the Englishwoman with the conventional accent, the blind fiancée, the blacks, the whalebone corset statue rolling along calves' marrow rails, the zither-playing earthworm, the Alcott brothers.

Nonetheless it has been our daily delight to go to the Théâtre Antoine. People were laughing, whistling, "get-it-offing". The actors themselves frequently aligned themselves with the audience and this unexpected communication between stage

time will **Impressions d'Afrique** perhaps be hailed as another masterpiece? Who knows?   −Noziere

and theatre was truly delicious.

M. Dorival was a sublime King Talou. He played the role forty times and forty times he obtained new and unimpeachable effects.

He left this glorious role with infinite regret. Yesterday, before the curtain could be lowered upon the last act, he struck his chest and cried "Vive les Français!" Thus ended the delightful careeer of this gay play which we hope to see again, for our enjoyment and our education."
−(uncredited newspaper notice), 11th June, 1912.

Dissappointed and puzzled by the indifferent or hostile reaction to the piece, Roussel came to the modest conclusion that the problem lay in his adaptation of the novel. Therefore he engaged Pierre Frondaie, a professional writer who specialised in adapting novels for the stage, to make a theatrical version of *Locus Solus*. The show opened at the Théâtre Antoine on December 8th 1922, with music by Maurice Fouret, décors by Emile Bertin and costumes by Paul Poiret, and closed after ten performances on December 21st:

A,e,i,o,u, drum, Central Africa, hydrogen peroxide, cigarette paper, Napoleon 1st, little salt spoon, the platform of a bus, Petrograd, **tzim, tzim, la tzim, la boum,** peanut, Cote d'Azur, cannibal, Mandel, phylloxera, Sarah Bernhardt, l, m, n, o, p, q, awoouh!, "bonjour Madame".

At the male emerald, the public grew angry and whistled. Money was thrown at the actors, in forty sou pieces.

The missile passed so close to Erbaf (Saturnin Fabre) that his hat fell off and he leapt backwards in surprise. But

Contrary to what I had been told, the stage show amused me far more than what was going on in the theatre. The glances I directed at the stalls did not afford any

(. . .) We have written the incoherent lines that you have just read, only because it seems to us that nothing could be better suited than they to give you an approximate idea of the incoherence of the work which we have just witnessed.
−Max and Alex Fisher, Dec. 9th, 1922

Signoret was injured.

Bewildered, he came up to the prompter's box. In a tearful voice, he implored the public to:

"Throw notes!"
−Saturnin Fabre, **Douche Ecossaise**

surprise glimpse of physiognomic indignation or admiration: I saw only open mouths, astonished eyes, dumbfounded ears. In the dress circle the public was

A scene from Locus Solus.

Canterel as played by Signoret.

neither more numerous nor less well-behaved. A moment came when someone or other of them decided to laugh. This phenomenon began towards the end of the first act. The "claque" (hired clappers) had already manifested its presence on several occasions without provoking the

least protestation. But, when it emphasised the last scene of the first act, a powerful voice cried: "Sham!"; another stentor added: "It's absurd!", and a third: "To the nuthouse!"
— R. Millet, **L'Avenir**, 18th Dec. 1922

I demand the creation of a police force of theatrical morals to prevent the

return of similar scandals.
—Louis Schneider, **La Suisse**, 14 Dec. 1922

Francois Caradec[4] recounts how audiences became factionalized, with Roussel's band of young supporters so vigorous as to disrupt *La Guerre à Pantoufles*, a short one act play by Gabriel Timmory and Félix Galipaux, which had been added to the bill after cuts had been made to *Locus Solus* itself:

"André Breton, Aragon, Francis Picabia, Robert Desnos, Georges Auric, Josephson, and Michel Leiris, armed with complimentary tickets, returned on the night of the public premiere, the 11th December. They dispersed throughout the theatre and ceaselessly applauded and exclaimed in loud voices. Exasperated, the spectators ended up challenging them. But during *La Guerre a Pantoufles*, the dadaists went wild.

They booed, yelled: "Stupid", "It's a fake": allusions to patriotic sentiment were greeted with vociferations: "Down with France! Long live Germany!", an actor's interrogative "Well?" fell into silence, Aragon launched from the circle "Well, shit!" On this occasion the directorate of the theatre, which was not yet used to this sort of thing, called the police. The actors joined with the spectators to protest against the perturbators—who were defending Roussel's play!"

Roussel's private wealth became the target for attacks by critics and others either too outraged or too lazy to deal with the play:

M. Roussel is not the only one who professes that "Maecaenism (5) begins at home!" Oronte (6) overwhelms us and the theatre is nothing more than a millionaire's plaything. I've been told that M. Roussel dispensed crazy sums of money to stage for us the pretentious idiocy that he

has entitled **Locus Solus**. He guaranteed the participation of great artists, who must have been grossly overpaid to be the performers of such a poverty-stricken work!
—Pierre Veber, 9th Dec.

"There is good to be done"

. . . Is the eccentric author really sure that he could not dispose more agreeably of the enormous sums which he is pleased to throw away on the stage, at the risk of not being very favourably judged? . .

Has the eccentric author not read the recent and moving appeal launched in aid of French science? . . Has he never heard talk of the misery of poor people with family responsibilities, of the distress of our students, of the sombre desolation of the unemployed?

Has he never met a beggar?

Did he not read yesterday, in the Gaulois, the heart-rending story of a visit made to the noble old poet Maurice de Plessys? On the seventh floor of a dreary house, in an icy garret, the poet, completely paralysed, lies on a bed, alone . . . His wife, who runs a newspaper kiosk, leaves at dawn and returns at night. And there are two children to feed. And there is the paralytic . . .

Ah! do good, do good! . . . That must be far more comforting, deep down—and even more agreeable and more joyful! . . . —than stupidly to create a folly on the stage.

—Maurice Prax, **Petit Parisien,** 10th Dec.

"A Protest by the General Association of Students"

Many students are actually in extreme poverty and, for want of a few francs, are unable to eat their fill.

A quidam, who no doubt believes himself an intellectual, has found a million to mount an ineptitude: **Locus Solus.**

The public evaluated the work at its correct worth: however there were some people placed in the theatre to applaud (without irony).

You will judge the tone of the play by knowing that it begins with the convey ance on stage of a coffin into which the pall-bearers pour a liquid to cool the cadaver.

To spend such a sum at this time for a manifestation of this type is rather like throwing a piece of bread in the gutter.

And it is really insulting to try to suppress the protestations of the public under the pretext of the consideration due to the talented performers who are playing.

Those actors are to be pitied! Shouldn't we resolve to send such harum-scarums to the **Cloaque Maxime?**

This provoked one of the few really considered pieces of critical writing about *Locus Solus*:

An injustice is an injustice; it is no less hateful when done to Croesus than when done to Diogenes; and, where literature is concerned, the obligation to protest the fact is equally imperative.

A writer has written a play; everything indicates that he has followed his heart in writing it; he has the very natural desire to have it performed; it is well known that it is difficult to break through the gates of the great Parisian theatres; M. Raymond Roussel reckons he has no chance in succeeding in this; now he is born rich, even very rich, it is said; he tells himself that the simplest thing would be to cover the performance costs himself. I know a writer who, born not in the least rich, and also despairing of having his work performed, preferred to use the money which he had been able to win, to rent a theatre and engage some actors. There is, after all, no difference between this and the practice of the majority of young poets when they publish their first book of verse at their own expense. But M. Roussel (if he will forgive me saying so) is not an adroit millionaire; not only does he not know how to defend himself, but he makes himself the object of excessive exploitation; he tolerates the ridiculous publicity made of him; through simplicity (which is evident) and without knowing it (which less evident) he makes ostentation; by which I mean that, all around his work, the sniff of money is circulating, heaps of money. It is precisely the naivety of his blunder that, in my eyes, pleads in his favour, but it exasperates the crowd; this incompetence in the use of his fortune, this total incomprehension of Parisian susceptibilities—one cannot imagine more disastrous conditions in which to produce a play; which takes place; and what happens to it? Before knowing a line of it, before hearing a word of it, the critics' attitude is formed and, with them, that of the famous dress-rehearsal public . . . If you write a favourable article, word will get around that you were paid; I am not talking about the uncomprehending and rancorous anger of a few who would very much liked to be paid! Amongst the others, I mean the honest people, this sentiment exists (explicable in short) that this gentleman must not imagine that, just because he is rich and because he has spent money . . . And the best critics pull it to pieces, or remain silent.

Well, although this is very human, it is abominable that there has not been a single person (at least to my knowledge) who has listened to **Locus Solus** with the same ear as that with which one would hear the work of an ordinary writer.

—Edouard Dujardin, **Révue de l'Époque**, May 1923.

Dujardin's commonsense approach led him logically to the novel, " . . . having seen the play, I wanted to read the novel; it was an immense surprise to me. In the novel there was no trace of the buffoonery which had enchanted me in the play", which suggests that the adaptation was not very faithful to the original text. Descriptions of the staging tend to support this idea:

The costumes, the work of (Paul) Poiret, were extremely witty. They were conceived in the **dadaist** style, from which the artistic side was by no means excluded . . .

—Albert de Peyronnet, 9th Dec

It was all lost on M. Antoine himself (after whom the theatre was named):

"Am I awake?"

You are familiar with the kind of small scandal caused by the performance of a play so incoherent that it begs the question whether or not the author simply set out to see just how far the gaping and patience of the Parisian public can go? Well, this chap, who is not in on the secret of the experience, and who bore the cost of it, ended up by getting angry; after two hours of grim **ennui**, in the face of such aggressive puerility, he finally woke up, and poor Signoret knew something about it.

And what the devil was he doing there?

Unlike so many of his comrades, he doesn't have the excuse of having to earn a living at all costs; he has just returned from a fruitful South American tour and is not short of big engagements in Paris; this is a grave imprudence on his part, all the more infuriating when one recalls that it was on this stage that he won his first stripes.

To judge fairly the responsibilities, it would be necessary to know the circumstances which could have led to this spectacle being staged; here we find the mercantilism which, little by little, is strangling our poor theatre.   —9th Dec

But there were those who attacked the play while grudgingly acknowledging the power of its imagery:

Locus Solus does not tell a story, having neither beginning nor end. It's all about calve's marrow rails, whalebone corset carriages, asthmatic Majors who are cured by breathing into their aglets . . . and therein lies a sort of dismal frenzy of the absurd to which I confess I was not totally insensible.
—Francois Mauriac, **Université de Paris**, 23rd Dec. 1922

Now Roussel became convinced that his lack of critical success was due to the fact that his stage works had been adaptations of novels, and so he wrote his first play, *L'Etoile au Front*, which was staged at the Théâtre du Vaudeville between May 5th and 7th, 1924, for three performances only. This time the critical reaction began in advance of the performances, and the public came ready for a riot:

A new play by Raymond Roussel! This promises us an interesting battle between the "advanced" who praise the author of Locus Solus to the skies, and the traditionalists who are still scared by his boldness.
—**Avant-première**, 4th May

Roussel . . . had taken care to inform the General Association of Students in advance that two hundred seats would be at the disposal of students who wished to applaud his work at the Vaudeville.
They came, many of them, and greeted M. Roussel's three acts with vociferations.
One spectator, seated in the dress-circle, tried to stand up to them and, after the performance, he had it out with one of them in the corridors.

This young student, not without a certain pluck, withstood a group of the author's supporters, while his comrades loudly voiced their regret for the eighteen sous which they had spent on the bus ride to see L'Etoile au Front. One of them even pretended that it was a web under the forehead (la toile sous le front)—a spider's web.
—Uncredited report, 9th May 1924

In the second act, MM. Gabriel Boissy and Paul Gregorio began to protest, M. Gregorio cried: "What about the twins? I want to see the twins! There must be twins in the theatre!"
Stimulated, a voice cried out: "And the monkey?"
"Now look here," said M. Paul Lombard, phlegmatically. "You know very well that the author doesn't come on till the end!"
"I'm p...ing off out of here," Paul Gregorio declared. "If you lot don't do the same then you're a bunch of cretins!"
—**Aux Ecoutes**, 11th May 1924

M. Roussel was delighted. He was wearin the biggest smile and saying: "Yes, yes . . ., ca va ..., I'm happy . . ." And modestly he added: "Only there's still the third act to come isn't there?"

In the third act the place exploded. M. Boissy yelled: "They're taking the p... out of us!"
A young energumen (7) of the dadaist type stood up to him in the stalls.

Armed officers entered the fray. But the youth would not let them throw him out: "Let me stay in the theatre," he shouted, "seeing as I'm the only person defending the author."

—Aux Ecoutes, 11th May

The murmur rapidly developed into a clamour. The clamour became a storm. In the stalls, in the boxes, in the dress circle, everywhere. M. Roussel's little comrades, all of tender years, all arrogantly cretinous enough to make the new generation look ridiculous, were letting out unbelievable war-cries. The grumblers retorted. Near to me a little old man stood on the tips of his shiny ankle-boots like some farmyard bird and, each time that Yonnel ended his story, yelped out in a high pitched voice: "Another! Another!"

A bit further away, a nearly enraged spectator cupped his two black hands in front of his mouth and roared like a demon: "The bill! The bill!", his hair was standing on end.

—Jean Botrot, **Comoedia**, 7th May

In the middle of the first act, a voice was raised in the circle: "I don't understand."

From one of the stalls a gentleman replied: "Go and get an interpreter."

The scene recurred several times: "I don't understand," said the dress-circle gentleman, in a more and more dismal tone of voice. "Go and get an interpreter," insisted the man in the stalls, in a voice like a loudspeaker.

(. . .)

It got to a point when the atmosphere had become stormy. People were whistling from above.

Desnos (8) stood up: "Shut up, you c...."

The high society who Raymond Roussel had invited, were baffled as much by the play as by the public's response.

"Oh! The hooligan, the layabout. How beastly!"

The whistlers were more direct: "C... yourself."

"Come here and say that."

"You just wait, we're coming."

"Come on then."

While the actors waited patiently on stage, a great noise of downrush could be heard. It was the spectators from the circle and the gallery hurling themselves in a whirlwind upon Desnos. The surrealists yelled, the ladies died of fright.

A little old gentleman in a dress-coat, with a légion d'honneur ribbon, said to Robert: "Come over close to me, young man."

Robert stepped over the three rows of stalls, and stood beside the frail little old man who grabbed him by the jacket collar, forced him into a sitting position, protecting him with his thin silhouette, and declaring: "Come and get him!"

There followed a scrum, like in rugby. Therese, very worried, looked for Robert, at the same time delivering some thumps herself, for she was a coach at Hebert's.

Robert threw himself to the ground, and, in this posture, crawling on hands and knees, succeeded in getting out of the theatre by passing between the combatants legs. Thérèse followed him. Once outside, they took up positions on the pavement facing the theatre, and awaited the outcome of events. The safety curtain had been lowered, the police called and the theatre evacuated.

A lady in evening dress threw herself upon Desnos, shouting: "There he is, that vulgar fellow. I recognise him," and she gave him a slap in the face.

Robert, shrewdly, was careful not to retort in front of the crowd . . .

The police took several people, chosen at random, to the police station, and everybody dispersed.

—Youki Desnos, **Les Confidences de Youki**

The critics were no less violent, with M. Antoine leading the way:

"Too much patience"

The day before yesterday, at a matinée in one of our great Parisian theatres, we witnessed a small scandal which it is worth the trouble of noting (. . .)

An amateur author who has money hands it over all the more willingly to some lucky organizers so as to see it reflected back at him, so the press will come and see his work, and so that it will be discussed just like a regular show, even though it has only two or three virtually private performances, which, consequently, the real public cannot see. And we are invited to a commonplace, almost entirely useless, show, because a certain gentleman has the means to finance his little diversion. It's an increasingly frequent abuse of our goodwill and our patience.

For my part I will not talk about the play in question, and that's what we should always do; silence is the only means to combat the kind of practices which are steadily increasing the present confusion in which the theatre is struggling.

—Antoine, **Journal**, 7th May

Two years later Roussel's second play *La Poussière de Soleils*, was staged at the Théâtre de la Porte Saint-Martin. Once again he tried to win critical acclaim: the new play now had a clear plot, linking dialogue, and an absence of "bizarre" happenings on stage. Unfortunately this had the effect of alienating his erstwhile supporters, and disappointing audiences and critics, who were relishing the opportunity for another scandal:

The announcement of a new play by Raymond Roussel has provoked such a surge of curiosity that there is competition for the invitations.

—Press Notice, 2nd Feb.

For the creation at the Porte Saint-Martin (. . .) Raymond Roussel had rented the theatre at twice the normal price. And the fees alloted to the actors were fabulous. For three day's work an actor could receive the sum of three thousand francs from the patron.

During the rehearsals only the author was present. But the actors played as if the theatre was packed for this decent man whose generosity was a delight (. . .)

The day of the dress rehearsal M. Raymond Roussel distributed little sealed envelopes containing 10% more than the promised fee. This was so the creators of his work could purchase a small souvenir.

—**Le Panurge**, 11th Aug. 1933

I listened to individuals as they left the theatre: "What a disappointment!" they were saying. "The author's lost his bite; he's written an almost reasonable play, which is not even irritating. Now there's no more fun to be had!" And it's true, the public at the **Générales** were disappointed;

they came with the intention of making a row, of protesting! They were forced to drop that idea, the work was so uneventful; we're a long way from the calves' marrow rails and the one-legged man playing the flute on his tibia.

—Pierre Veber (9), **Petit Journal**, 4th Feb.

In his previous "works", M. Raymond Roussel has at least shown a certain charentonesque fantasy. This time his lunacy has got worse: it has become reasonable.

—**Le Théâtre et Comoedia illustré**, 1st June

M. Raymond Roussel's last play was somewhat disappointing, for it was very well-behaved, almost clear, hardly baroque at all. During the entr'acte the surrealists cubists, dadaists, who were there in the hope of a good storm, made no secret of their disappointment.

—**Aux Ecoutes**, 14th Feb.

A small number of critics made favourable comments, most noticeably Louis Laloy:

The interest of this show does not let up for a moment, and its stylistic qualities are pushed to a point which denotes a rare mastery.

—**L'Etre Nouvelle**, 4th Jan.

The play was performed three times, on February 2nd, 3rd and 5th 1926, to an invited audience. The following year it was revived for fifteen performances, beginning on 12th January 1927, at the Théâtre de la Renaissance. This time the reaction was more vigorous:

. . . Yesterday evening at the Théâtre de la Renaissance, lively protestations were to be heard in the middle of the second act of **Poussiere de Soleils**. Many of the troublemakers were expelled and the performance was able to end normally after their enforced departure,

—**Presse**, 20th Jan.

But this was not the kind of reaction that Roussel wanted. Michel Leiris poignantly recalled the final *échec*:

"Despite his constant disappointments, he missed none of the performances of his plays. However, in the course of a stormy evening in the Renaissance, during *La Poussière de Soleils*, he left the theatre before the end of the show, declaring that he could not take any more; in fact he never attended any other performance after that." [10]

Notes

1. *Comment j'ai écrit certains de mes livres*, p.19 of the Trevor Winkfield translation [Trans. note]
2. Quoted in Francois Caradec, *Vie de Raymond Roussel*, p. 112 [Trans.]
3. The quotations in this article are mostly taken from Francois Caradec's *Vie de Raymond Roussel*, Pauvert, Paris, 1972, and a few from *Bizarre*, No. 34/35, Paris, 1964. [Trans. note]
4. Caradec, op. cit., p. 219. [Trans.]
5. 'Maecaenism'—"rich patronage", after Maecanas, patron of Horace & Virgil. [Trans.]
6. 'Oronte'—a fop in Moliere's *Le Misanthrope*, who writes a sonnet in a quarter of an

hour and seeks applause. [Trans.]

7. 'energumen'— a fanatical devotee. [Trans.]

8. Robert Desnos, whose retort *Nous sommes la claque et vous etes la joue!* (We are the slap and you are the cheek! But *claque* also means the 'hired clappers') to those who were haranguing Roussel's supporters so delighted the latter that he commissioned Henri Zo to paint a diptych showing the riots at *L'Etoile au Front* and at the premiere of Hugo's *Hernani*, with Desnos' remark inscribed on a plaque. [Trans.]

9. Veber had been vicious in his criticism of Roussel's work in the past, yet Roussel immediately sent him a dedicated copy of *Impressions d'Afrique* and the following letter:

"How happy I am, dear M. Pierre Veber, that your charming article allows me to tell you, as I have wanted to for a long time without daring, how much I adore your plays, which I regularly go to see a dozen times. Every Thursday last winter, I attended the matinée of *Monsieur de cinq heures* in the same box (I assure you that the clerk knows my chauffeur well, he has the responsibility of booking it). I only interrupted this during the period when Monsieur Le Gallo was replaced. This summer, during a round trip I saw *Monsieur de cinq heures* in a town to the east, in Nancy, I believe.

A warm thank you for your tireless appreciation,

Raymond Roussel"   [Trans.]

10. Quoted in Caradec, op. cit., p.305. [Trans.]

ROBERT DE MONTESQUIOU
A Difficult Author

Translation   Catherine Allan

A publisher—a hard-hearted, disagreeable, and one must admit, narrow-minded man, but one who, when all is said and done, was perhaps well-acquainted with his business—once told me "a book that fails to sell itself immediately will never succeed in doing so later on." This unsubtle elucidation of popular taste could, in certain circumstances, be expressed more delicately in this fashion: Carmen's experience is not relevant in the domain of the book.[1] A volume cannot pass unnoticed or be coldly received, and then awaken to belated success and eventual triumph. It is irritating, alas, but probably true (...).

★

I do not know if Monsieur Raymond Roussel's book, so inadequately entitled *Impressions d'Afrique* (by an author who certainly does not lack the imagination to find a better one), experienced what is called success and met with intelligent notices.[2] It would not surprise me if the opposite were true, and this is one of the reasons that induces me, tardily—since by a happy circumstance I have only just become acquainted with the work two years[3] after its publication—to dedicate several lines to it, for I found it both interesting and entertaining.

Will the author be at least a little grateful for this, I don't know, and this would not now deter me from my purpose. There are authors and there are books. Sometimes the two are one and the same, at other times they do not make a pair. (...) I doubt whether *Impressions d'Afrique* will have attracted many academics to Monsieur Roussel's cause, and I conclude from this that my essay will leave him less than indifferent.

It is truly the Academy of Science, above all, that should have been interested in this traveller's tale, which is more than strange, ultra fantastical, and in the course of which a succession of mechanical devices appear, closely followed by their phenomenal consequences. It is not up to me to foretell whether these machines will remain in the domain of fantasy or whether the future has reserved for them the prospect of one day achieving an inventor's patent. What I can say is that they have diverted me, and as far as I am

Roussel in Carlsbad, 1910.

concerned, I here and now, as far as it is within my powers, bestow *that* patent upon them.

And I add this almost with regret, but the truth obliges me to admit it— I am not the only one, Monsieur Roussel has another admirer whose name is so well known that I will guard carefully against revealing it; my own would disappear in the glare of so blinding a fame.[4]

★

Let us approach the tessitura of this tome, at once scientific, musical and abracadabrical. It is divided into two parts. The first takes up half of the volume, and presents us with a series of performances at a gala, most of the actors being Europeans, on the occasion of the crowning of a negro king. Each of the absolutely original acts (take my word for it) of this startling festival, is stamped with the seal of mystery and the imprint of an enigma which eventually, after I know not how many hours have passed, leaves the spectator both bewildered and astonished by the presence of so much serious-ness united with such horse-play. One ends up in a curious state of mind, a mixture of reserved admiration and barely contained hilarity.

I well know that this can be called *humour*, but there are degrees of humour, as there are of vice and virtue, and, in the event, the degrees have be-come notches on a cog, and I assure you this is the last notch the mind can bear before cracking apart.

The second half of the work explains everything, not merely with satisfying logic, better than that, with a mathematical precision. The author says some-where of one of his characters, "the sum of his orations presented a great unity." This judgement could be applied to his narratives. The maddest in-coherencies of the preceding chapters are explained with a geometric exacti-tude and with such an equilibrium of corroborating evidence that it almost becomes monotonous. It seems they must represent the *hoc erat in votis* of this particular genre. It ends up giving these combinations, which are above all else eccentric and bizarre, a bourgeois appearance.

So we discover—and here I can only outline briefly the overall structure of this composition, at once spontaneous, extravagantly redundant and care-fully thought out—that the aforesaid performances have been organized by a group of shipwrecked passengers who have fallen into the hands of a barbarous sovereign who has compelled them to send his ransom demands to their families. They employ the days waiting for a reply by making use in this way, of the disparate talents of the hostages and the various cargoes

The celebrated portrait of Robert de Montesquiou by Boldini, 1897.

carried by the ship. I will not describe any of the phases of this *seria* and *buffa* opera, an opera without precedent, alas! and one which also lacks a future place in the histories of literature. No, this would lead me far from my path. I am content to refer the text to those who are dissatisfied with the shows announced daily in the illustrated columns of *Comœdia* and *Theatra*. I will only make certain observations on the totality of the work, the apparency it presents in its descriptions, and the enigma which is offered by its conclusions.

This last reservation brings me exactly to what I wish to say with regard to the theatrical presentation of this work. And it is here alone that the reader finds himself embarassed, when the reader is myself. I doubt whether anyone else has penetrated to any extent the intentions of the author who seemingly shares that taste for chilly mystifications with that school of English writers, whose almost algebraic passion is for posing equations of events which appear insoluble, and which they then proceed to unravel with an apparent ease which leaves no place for questions. It is all done by making a speciality out of throwing perilous pirouettes in the air and allowing them to fall to earth again, sometimes gracefully, or at least in the centre of a net prudently extended beneath, which prevents fatal accidents. All this leaves me not only without rebellion, but also without objection and even, I must admit, somewhat acquiescent. But where I admit I don't understand at all—for it would mean the author possessed a mentality absolutely irreconcilable with many of the fine ironic touches in his stories—is when I hear he has written an outrageous adaptation of his book and put it on the boards in a very gorgeous production, with a luxuriant multiplicity of posters, and an evident desire to see it become a popular success.

I cannot refute the solutions to any of the impossibilities posed and finally solved in his book, but this last I defy anyone to explain to me.

A writer, at once tremendous and delicate, delights in the melancholic hauteur of composing works such as those of which Bauderlaire said, "I call them famous because they are appreciated by me and some of my friends"—nothing could be better, it denotes a character which, when associated with talent, commands attention or at least respect. But to believe that the curiosity of M. Prevost's faithful audience or the spectators of *Le Cœur dispose* could be attracted to such works, there arises a misunderstanding, to some extent ingenuous, which amidst all the illusions, spells, and tricks of Monsieur Roussel, is the only one that finds me rebellious, obstinate, uncomprehending, and I defy him to explain his reasons to me.

It is also true, so I am told, that the stage of the *Femina* has twice served as the place in which a scenic adaptation has occurred, which was remounted and I believe prolonged in another Parisian theatre, and finally made a tour of France. In spite of which, and apart from certain facile jibes and impulsive criticisms, I have been unable to obtain any information on these manifest-ations, only that the author participated in person, sometimes as an actor, sometimes directing events sitting right in the middle of the room.

If, despite my admiration for Madame Garnier, I only feebly regret the thought that I will have to die without having seen *La Bonne Intention*, on the other hand, I cannot console myself that a relative distance and partial retreat deprived me from being present at the visible, creaking and jumpy transposition of *Impressions d'Afrique.*

I will therefore refrain from formulating an opinion of a play which I have not seen. But I have read a book, and it is that I wish to consider and to speak a few more words.

★

They will contain a second objection which bears precisely upon the title which I reproach for simply being a sub-title. Why (it's certainly not due to a lack of imagination) did he not fasten upon these five hundred pages of delirious and erudite fantasy a plume as original as the multiplicity of bizarre head-dresses which empurple and leap out from so many of its pages. Just the memory of these dictates to me titles which already exist, such as, for example "The Incomparables Club", the name chosen by the performers themselves for their collection of 'phenomena'; or again, "The Gardens of the Behuliphruen", the poetic name of the nearby walkway along which many of the performers' twists of fortune unfold, during their exiled promenades. But a vital attraction is missing in this unformed title, it was precisely up to the Author not to deprive his work of it, and only he could have devised the necessary and absent vocable in keeping with his original composition.[5]

Despite this abovementioned reservation, I should stress the comic aspect, happening always cursorily or almost at the whim of chance, which I have discovered in these inventions. Like the child negro prince who, cruel and pitiless as his years, allows the freed prisoners to keep their loose change, which counts for nothing against the ransoms demanded. These latter profit by the presence among them of two financiers by creating a stock exchange in miniature, or rather caricature, in which they play every day, the hypothetical values being represented by each other and by their future potentialities. Thus we see shares in a young male acrobat, whose talent is mounting an exhibition of performing cats, rising to sixty francs; whereas those of an old Livonian ballerina, who is vainly attempting to resuscitate her past gracefulness, fall piteously to sixty centimes.

This is followed by an excellent satire on present day intellectuality. A great tragedienne involved in the ship-wreck has discovered, hidden in an English castle, the actual manuscript of the first version of "Romeo and Juliet", of course it is entirely different from the one currently in favour. The actress takes it to all the directors in the world, offering to interpret the part, they all refuse with indignation. Sadly impassioned, the artist profits by her stay among the blacks by having the authentic first thoughts of Shakespeare, which have been rejected unanimously by those managers responsible for all the great theatres of the civilised world, performed perfectly by a couple of charming savages.

Such an episode ensures that the author of *Impressions d'Afrique* will take precedence over the author of "Lord Rutland is Shakespeare". The latter has merely discovered that Shakespeare isn't Shakespeare. The former has invented a Shakespeare who is more than Shakespeare.

But what also carries his wonderful satires forward is the comic effect that is offered us every day, as blatantly as you like, in the contemplation of those photographs taken by travellers in which decorative objects, that glitter and shine, are placed in the hands of blacks to hold. So we see, even here, a Dinah Salifou asking the Maison Poussielgue (or some other ecclesiastical supplier) for copes and mitres destined for prelates to put themselves in the ministry. Similarily, Monsieur Roussel's African heros and males choose their costumes from European engravings and fashion plates, from the dresses of Marguerite in *Faust*, or the actresses in Revue.

In the end, everything is sorted out, the prisoners are freed, they re-embark joyously with their belongings, exchanging cordial farewells when they get to their ports of respective repatriations. But among the 'phenomena' a limbless man is to be found, gifted with good humour and talent despite his lack of extremities. So the Barnum concludes his gaudy performance with good-humoured, sensitive and compassionate bathos, "The crossing was accomplished without incident, and on the 19th. July we took leave of each other on the quayside at La Joliette, after a cordial exchange of handshakes, from which only Tancrede Boucharessas [this is the freak's name] had to remain a stranger."

★

What characterises this singular work is his love for that type of literary logogriph which explains itself later on; a taste for taking events to pieces, and throwing the pieces in a hat (be it the most surprising of 'bowlers') then reassembling them at the end into a perfect jig-saw puzzle. This preference appears to be so dominant in Monsieur Roussel's works, that it seems to me to be the reason (at least to a great extent) for his embarking into literature: he wanted *to read this*, and since no other author could provide it, he became *his own reader*. I admire this attitude. Perhaps, after all Monsieur Bourget and Monsieur Prevost may have preserved within themselves enough good taste to become bored with amusing so many people.

And when I say *jig-saw*, I could just as well have written *'casse-tete'*[6], so long as one attends to all the implications of this word—the difficulties of the Chinese game, the fine and crafted ornamentation of the counters, lozenges of pearl or squares of ivory, with which it is played.

The work reminds me also of a Japanese game, in which tiny, shapeless shavings of wood are created so they open up in hot water, and the liquid makes them blossom into flowers, birds or insects, coloured and sinuous.

The style of this wager, which has successively taken on the aspect of a book and of a play, is perfectly suited to its serious and grotesque vision. I have found nothing in need of being re-written in the course of so long a reading. It is doubtless deliberate, his eschewal of poetic effects. His descriptions are sober, but have a nicety of expression that is consistent and complete, it achieves all he wishes to say, be it scientific or impressionistic.

Certainly the author has read Wells and the Villiers of *L'Eve Future*, he has their dogmatic, professional and grotesque tone, and certain of these fantasies give me, exotically, an equivalent pleasure to that I found previously in the reading of *Les Oiseaux s'envolent* by Elemir Bourges. Also certain of Huysmans' transcriptions of thoughts, from *La bas*, if I'm not mistaken, return to me in spirit, while reading such and such a passage of the ordered nightmare which is the art of Raymond Roussel. But all this is amalgamated with a split personality in which I can see but one inconsistency, which is the one I have mentioned.

Howsoever that may be, what remains with me from the hours spent in the company of this itinerary, is the curious flavour of a *recipe* based on couscous which paradoxically reconciles the contrasting aromas of angelica and paprika, of curry and cinnamon, of cloves and cumin, of barberry and of musk.

—1921

Notes

1. Bizet's "Carmen" only achieved its phenomenal popularity some years after an initially bad reception.
2. In fact, to some extent, it did. Francois Caradec (*Vie de Raymond Roussel,* pps. 104-7) gives several examples of the stupefied, but generally favourable, reactions of the critics.
3. Now many more. [Author's note] Presumably therefore the first draft of this essay was written around 1912.
4. The "other admirer" is almost certainly Edmond Rostand, the playwright.
5. Caradec gives various Rousselian interpretations of the title (op. cit., p. 100):

    The "Impressions" of Africa derive from "the letters of the white man about the blacks" in *Parmi les Noirs,* but they are also "impressions" in the sense of printed impressions, i.e. impressions of black (letters) on white (paper). He also suggests another reading of the title:

    1. *Impressions* (sensations) d' (of) *Afrique* (the continent).
    2. *impression* (printed) a (at) *fric* (the author's expense).

    All Roussel's works were indeed printed at his own expense.
6. "Casse-tete", literally "break-head", a Chinese puzzle or tangram.

THÉÂTRE ANTOINE

DORIVAL

"IMPRESSIONS D'AFRIQUE"

Le Bureau de Location est ouvert de 11 h. du matin, a 6 h. du soir. Location 1 fr. de plus par place.

Téléphone 436.32

PHILIPPE SOUPAULT
Raymond Roussel

Translation   Antony Melville

Does the chance rediscovery of the rules of the game, and joyless calculation, provide an answer to the mute questioning of railway and shipping lines? I find this doubt, this dead weight of concern which hangs over our lives like the fear of accidents, or the horror of being knocked down, at every step in *Impressions d'Afrique.*

The silent sympathy on the one hand, and the respectful antipathy on the other, which surround Roussel, can be explained by the author's wealth. In spite of the perjorative sense attached to this word when applied to a writer, it is not a meaningless statement to say that Raymond Roussel is rich. And I do not think it is a lie to add that his fortune comes from his parents. The special up-bringing he received, and the theatrical events of his childhood served to reinforce an inclination which is the privilege of those *whose only pain was that of birth*: the inimitable pleasure of watching the agitation of others—be they animals, humans or machines. Not every man can take an interest in these games, these labours. Enthusiasts for sporting events are either sportsmen or professionals of luck.

Roussel possesses this taste to a very high degree. He indulges it fearlessly in his book. He imagines new effects, sensational machines, superhuman feats, which he describes like a De Chirico, and a specialist. To this incredibly keen taste is added the desire for risk. All the combinations he erects are at the mercy of a single moment of distraction. When danger takes wing like a wounded bird in the spontaneous silence, when the life of a man trembles for an instant, mirroring itself, like a star on the end of a thread, a heart stops: eyes glaze over and the stupefaction has begun.

The task of transferring this pleasure (without for a moment slipping into exoticism) to a country beneath the leaden sun of West Africa, where nature is alone bearable, where cruelty prowls, is what Roussel achieves, with a hint of affectation, in his *Impressions d'Afrique.*

Roussel chose this title with gratuitous irony. The gravity of his irony extends throughout the whole book. The author, who is a great traveller, adopts the attitude of readers of the *Journal des Voyages*: the African's love of glass beads, European clothes and watches. He discovers the public square, the fun-fair and the blandishments of charlatans. A street becomes a theatre, and men, despicable and despised, become clever animals, while the animals are better trained than the men.

Irony, usually a convenient mask, is the indispensible concomitant to stupidity. Mockery comes from the gizzards of the wretches who slowly lick up the dust which falls from heaven. I would pay that rabble to take their sarcasm somewhere else. But I would never suggest lumping Roussel with them. The irony that colours his books has the same tone as that which enflames *Une Saison en Enfer.* It allows him to put together the simplest combinations without weakness, and does not preclude either detective-story type mystery, or the reader's breathlessness as he turns the pages faster and faster. Having brought together the names of Rimbaud and Roussel, one could well continue this little game by linking the names of Gaston Leroux[1] and Raymond Roussel.

Amid the wind, the rain and the trees, shadows are moving. One can see them gliding about, but they remain indistinct. It is as if opera glasses or sometimes even long sight are required. They are men which the author describes as if they were little mechanical toys, like the ones his parents used to buy him on the *grands boulevards.* A vague disquiet runs through them whose object is even vaguer than disquiet and they are dominated by the fear of a tyrant. These poor toys know the elements only by name; fire and water follow the command of him who spoke last.

Impressions d'Afrique does not illustrate a geographical map, but the movement of a clock. I know a shop in Paris where old men painstakingly assemble the endless reflections of fantasy through the centuries. Everything is up-to-date and corresponds to the stream of joyful prattle in my mind. I can admire unreservedly these objects which only await my hands' caress. A single look sets off crystal mechanisms and unleashes torrents of papier-mache. I know not which idiot hanger-on who came to this happy spot with my friends and me, confided to me pleasantly and confidentially: "This shop makes me think of the poem by Arthur Rimbaud which starts:

I loved the maudlin paintings . . .[2]

Roussel took walks down this very boulevard a few years ago; at the time he was writing his *"impressions"* and he must have laughed as he admired this shop's window-display. It was not Rimbaud's poem it made him think of, but the first hundred pages of the book he was finishing." We are each of us free to share this obvious laughter. I cannot deny that for my part I find in his book the same pleasure as I do in the smell of this shop. Each object and each line are mingled with the minutes I am living and if I did not hesitate to use so worn a word I would confess that the atmosphere of *Impressions d'Afrique* is frankly "modern".

Writing, writing, it all amounts to the same thing. Is it still a question of arithmetic? One opens a window onto music paper and speaks of dynamism. To other people! Well, others speak of craft, of talent, and of the subjunctive.

Roussel answered in 1897 by publishing these lines:

Sometimes a momentary reflection comes to life
In the view set into the base of the pen-holder
Which my wide-open eye is pressed against
Very close, just fractionally back from it;
The view is let into a little ball
Of glass, which is still visible and makes
A glasshouse at the top of the white pen-holder
Where red ink has left stains as if of blood.
The view is a very slender photograph
Completely invisible if one relies
On the depth of the glass, this piece of which is frosted
On one of its sides, in this case the back;
But it all swells up when a more curious eye
Comes close enough for a lash at times to touch.
I am holding the pen-holder horizontal
With three fingers around its metal case
Which gives me a cool feeling where I touch;
My left eye firmly closed helps me to keep
My mind off other things, from being side-tracked
By other displays or some other attraction
That may arise outside, seen through the open
Window in front of me.

Weariness: hollow eyes, trembling hands, the curtains drawn, end of the day.

Haste does not give one time to lift one's head and search for hours. Roussel's poetry cannot be placed in everyone's hands. Typists and shipping clerks, you can expect to find it only useless prattle. In spite of its appearance this poetry is more hermetic and more difficult to approach than Mallarme's. It seems boring in many ways: it is in fact merely luxurious. One needs to be able to understand idleness and the charm of not knowing what to do with one's ten fingers.

Is it you, reader, who submit to repeating every morning and every evening "Where are we going?"

It is the poetry of an unoccupied and tuberculous man; this reader, for one, seeks in it total uselessness. That is why *La Doublure* (1896) and *La Vue* (1897) seem to me as tragically important as *Impressions d'Afrique*.

There is really nothing to believe. Roussel has no need of an apostle. Friendships are at the mercy of a thunderclap but never at the mercy of a swordthrust. It does not amount to the same thing.

"Keep the little children away from me," Roussel repeats, and turns his head away.

I take the liberty of comparing this poetic attitude with the more wilfully poetic one of our dear poets these days. Besides, Roussel always knew how to make use of publicity. A dozen years ago big posters appeared on the walls of Paris to announce performances of *Impressions d'Afrique* at the Theatre Antoine. I remember the astonishment of young telegraph operators who read out loud the surprising announcement of "rails made of calves' innards!"

Since then Roussel has wrapped himself in silence and gone away. He wrote to me in 1920 from Tahiti. I have in turn left him. It is no longer the time to speak of him. The first of us will await the other.

—1922

Notes

1. Gaston Leroux (1868-1927): popular French novelist, author of 'The Phantom of the Opera', 'The Mystery of the Yellow Room' and the splendid Captain Michel stories, among many others.
2. In fact the 3rd line from 'Delirium II', part of *Une Saison en Enfer.*

Dr. Pierre Janet
The Psychological Characteristics of Ecstasy

Translation   John Harman

The ecstasies of Plotinus, of Nietzsche and the famous ecstasy of J. J. Rousseau in the Bois de Vincennes are well-known; I refer to the fine descriptions of them given by M. Seillière. But I would like to bring to your attention one of my own case histories, to which I have often referred; that of Martial.[1] This forty-five year old man has led a most singular existence, he lives alone, in great seclusion, isolated in a way that seems very sad, but from which he derives great joy since he works almost constantly. He works, constructing great literary works, in a regular fashion for a fixed number of hours each day, not allowing himself the slightest deviation, with great effort and often to the point of exhaustion, "I shed blood over every phrase," he says. These literary works, whose worth I have not investigated, have had little success, they are unread and if one discounts those initiates[2] who are interested in them, they are considered to be insignificant. However, the author maintains a very unusual attitude toward them: not only does he continue his work with an untiring perseverance, but he is also absolutely convinced and steadfast as to their "immeasurable artistic value". The belief of an author in the value of his works and the appeal to posterity over the injustice of his contemporaries is natural and to some extent legitimate, but still it seems to me that Martial's conviction is abnormal. He attributes a disproportionate importance to his works, he is never shaken by their flagrant lack of success, he never admits for one moment that this failure may be justifed by certain imperfections, he never accepts the slightest criticism or advice, he has absolute faith in the fate reserved for him: "I shall reach great heights, I have been born for a blazing glory. It may take a long time, but I shall have greater glory than Victor Hugo or Napoleon. Wagner died twenty-five years too soon and never knew his own glory, but I hope to live long enough to contemplate my own . . . There lies within me an immensely powerful glory like a shell about to explode . . . This glory will be seen in every one of my works, and will reflect on all the acts of my life. People will research the acts of my childhood and admire the way I played 'prisoners' base'. No author has been, or can ever be greater than I, although no one is aware of this today: well, what can one expect—some shells explode belatedly, but when they do! . . . Whatever you may think, some are predestined! As the poet says: "And there are those who feel burning on their forehead . . . The resplendent star which they carry there."[3] These affirmations regarding works which do not seem destined to win a large readership and which have attracted so little attention, seem to indicate either a weakness of judgement or an exalted pride, combined with a state of great agitation. However, Martial does not deserve either reproach: he has sound opinions on all other matters and is certainly in all other respects of his behaviour, modest and even rather timid; far from being agitated, he is in a state of depression, with a tendency to obsessiveness and weakness of will. This conviction of glory is not related to a present psychological state, it is what remains of a psychological disorder from the past, which alone may explain it.

Martial, a young neuropath, timid, scrupulous, easily depressed, experienced at the age of nineteen, for five or six months, a mental condition that even he deems extraordinary. Taking up literature, which he preferred to the other pursuits he had followed up to that time, he undertook to write a great work in verse and wished to complete it before the age of twenty. Since this poem was to consist of several thousand verses,[4] he worked assiduously almost without ceasing, day and night, with no feeling of fatigue. He felt himself being gradually filled with a strange enthusiasm: "You feel something special when creating a masterpiece, that you are a prodigy: there are prodigous children who have revealed their talents at the age of eight—I have done so at nineteen. I was the equal of Dante and Shakespeare, I experienced what Victor Hugo felt at sixty-two, what Napoleon felt in 1811, and what Tannhauser dreamt at Venusberg: I experienced glory . . . No, glory is not an idea, a sentiment one acquires on hearing one's name play on the lips of strangers. No, it is not a question of feeling your own worth, or the conviction that you deserve glory. I never felt the need, or the desire for glory, since I never thought of it at all before. This glory was a fact, an affirmation, I had glory . . . Everything I wrote was surrounded in rays of light; I would close the curtains for fear the shining rays that were emanating from my pen would escape through the smallest chink; I wanted to throw back the screen and suddenly light up the world. To leave these papers lying about would have sent out rays of light as far as China and the desperate crowd would have flung themselves upon my house. But I did indeed have to take precautions, rays of light were streaming from me and penetrating the walls, the sun was within me and I could do nothing to prevent the incredible glare. Each line was repeated a thousand-fold and I wrote with a thousand flaming pen-nibs. No doubt, when the volume appeared, the blinding furnace would be revealed and illuminate the entire universe, but no one would believe that I had once contained it within myself . . . I was at that moment in a state of unheard-of bliss, one blow of the pick-axe had opened up a whole mine, I had won the most dazzling prize of all. I was more alive at that moment than at any other time of my whole existence." During this period Martial lost all interest in anything else and had great difficulty in interrupting his work in order to eat from time to time. He was not entirely motionless, he took a few steps, then wrote a little, but he remained immobile for hours on end, pen in hand, absorbed in his reverie and his sensations of glory.

This enthusiasm and these feelings lasted, with fluctuations, the entire time he was composing his verses, a period of five or six months; they diminished greatly during the printing of the book. When the volume appeared, as the young man with great emotion, went out into the street and realised that no one was turning to stare at him as he passed, the sensations of glory and luminosity were rapidly extinguished. There then began a real crisis of melancholic depression, taking the strange guise of persecution mania in the form of an obsession with and a delirious conception of, the universal denigration of men by each other. This depression lasted for a long time and healed very slowly, its traces remain even today.

However, from this crisis of glory and brilliance, Martial has kept the unshakeable conviction that he had glory, that he possessed it, whether men recognised him or not was of no importance. Concerning this he likes to quote a passage from M. Bergson's book *On Spiritual Energy*: "One clings to eulogy and honours in the exact proportion to which one is uncertain of having succeeded. There is insecurity at the bottom of vanity. It is to reassure oneself that one seeks approbation and it is perhaps to support an insufficient vitality in one's work that one seeks to surround it with the warm admiration of men, like swathing a premature infant in cotton-wool. But he who is certain, absolutely certain of having produced a viable and durable work has no concern for eulogy and feels himself above glory, because he knows that he has it, and because the joy he feels is a divine joy." Martial wrote other volumes it is true, but not in order to create something superior to the first, there is no progress in the absolute and from the very first he had the absolute of glory. These other works will only help the ignorant and behind-the-times public to read and grasp the shining light of the first.

He has indeed retained a second feeling, namely an intense desire, the mad passion to rediscover, as if they were but five minutes past, the sentiments that flooded his heart over those few months when he was nineteen. "Ah, that sensation of moral sunlight, I have never been able to find it again, I have sought it, and I shall forever seek it. I would give all my remaining years of life to relive one instant of that glory. I am Tannhauser looking back on Venusberg." He hopes that some effective success outside might be able to reanimate that internal sensation of glory, and it is for this reason that he attempts new books and abandons himself to further echoes of his first work. "But their success or failure are of little import: one retards the external realisation of his glory by others, while the other does not extinguish its reality."

There is much to say about this interesting case, but I only outline the points which bear similarities to the known facts about religious ecstasies. In these lay ecstasies, as in those of J. J. Rousseau, Nietzsche and Martial we discover the cessation of nearly all external activities, internal travail, the continuous recollection of the past event, the absolute faith which persists for years after the crisis, and above all an overwhelming joy. But there is not that great and solemn constancy of the ecstasy of J. J. Rousseau, which ebbs and flows, Martial leads a more or less normal life, appearing at one moment for a meal, the next shutting himself in a room, or sitting at table, but he works and composes verses endlessly. The subject retains his human interests, for after all, both politics and literary glory are dependant on the existence of ordinary citizens and readers, and he considers their actions and opinions important. The happiness he imagines is immense, but not very different to that which we ascribe to kings and famous writers, and it is not entirely novel. I would be inclined to say that these states, particularily that of Martial, are analogous to the consolations of Magdalen, coming out of ecstasy to her self-communion. Despite these differences, the content of the ideas are close to religous concepts, and has to do with western philosophy, idealistic politics, totally imaginary literature and pure artistic beauty. Martial has a very interesting conception of literary beauty, it is essential that a work should not contain anything real, no observations of the real or spiritual world, only entirely imaginary combinations, these are already the conceptions of a world beyond that of humanity. True ecstasy, constant and without self-interest, with a life and joy beyond ordinary human experience, must necessarily take a more religious form, conducive to a holy life, a life in God, a life of God.

_1926

Notes

1. From Martial Canterel, the hero of *Locus Solus*. The beginning of the next line allows us to date the writing of this article at around 1922, although it was published four years later. Roussel seems to have been consulting Janet since about 1897, soon after his 'crisis'.
2. "Those initiates" are the surrealists. A few years later Janet dismissed their works as "the writings of obsessed persons and doubters" during the dispute between parts of his profession and the surrealists over certain passages in Breton's *Nadja*.
3. I have been unable to trace the source of these lines. 'The Star on the Forehead' apart from being the title of his first play, is one of Roussel's most frequent images. Francois Caradec (*Vie de Raymond Roussel,* p. 42) lists many examples, but again does not give the identity of "the poet". The image seems connected, however, to Roussel's admiration for the astronomer and novelist Camille Flammarion. After Roussel's death, Dora Maar discovered in a Paris flea-market the object illustrated here: a star-shaped biscuit enclosed in a specially constructed glass box. The inscription reads: "Star from a meal taken on Sunday 29th. July, 1923, at the Juvisy Observatory with Camille Flammarion presiding. Raymond Roussel."

The drawing of a star scattered through the present volume is "The Star of Hope", an illustration from Flammarion's *Uranie,* one of Roussel's favourite books, from which he used to read aloud. An English version 'Urania' exists (trans. Augusta Stetson, Estes and Lauriat, Boston, 1890).
4. *La Doublure.*

ROGER VITRAC
Raymond Roussel

Translation   Kathleen Cannell & Antony Melville

This dramatist, celebrated henceforth for his failures, has been called: *The Chess Player.*

(Le Merle Blanc.)

On the 7th of December 1922... *he woke up and, having collected the elements which God... and 1922 put at his disposal, he organized the extravagantly improbable into three acts and six scenes, gave his final orders to* apparent absurdity... *and struck, twenty four hours late, the hour of hysterical laughter.*

This phrase ended the notice published in the papers on the morning of the first performance of *Locus Solus.* Already, the day before and for some preceding days, public opinion had been systematically prepared. Those who had not read the fabulous and logical narratives of the work with the same title, which Raymond Roussel had published some time back, were much intrigued by hearing of a *diamond bath-tub, unsalted fish that play at little horses, a musical tarot made of a male emerald, etc...* Everyone wanted to see and hear the nude dancer who spoke (*have you ever heard a nude dancer speak?*) He who had inspired these announcements was not unaware of the obscene stir provoked by the voice of a nude woman in movement, nor of the fact that music-hall audiences are ill at ease since the ordinance of a psychologist Chief of Police condemning nudes to immobility. And the most exigent spectator, whom the acting, the modern scenery, and the music of a young composer had failed to move, had to own his defeat when he learned that the great Gemier had accepted the manuscript before leaving the *Théâtre Antoine* for the *Odéon.* Today no one is ignorant of the fact that Pierre Frondaie had the rare privilege of adapting *Locus Solus* for the stage and that *L'Insoumise* was willing, at the height of its success, to submit to the exactions of the inventor *Canterel.*

The play will never appear in book form. It is a pity, for the most significant lines and the most violent invectives were dictated by Raymond Roussel, who insisted, regardless of scandal, that they be repeated to satiety. And he emphasized this note in a preliminary declaration:

"Apparent absurdity gives you food for reflection, logic dances a jig, the burlesque makes you split your sides laughing, but contains its moral lesson."

It would be, at least, amusing to analyze the collaborator's share in this work, to know how he was inspired to surpass himself in a genre not his own, almost to create it by the sole virtue of an atmosphere (as foreign to him as was l'*acqua micans* to the *Wine of Sauterne,* which it nevertheless transformed into a little sun) and how he was led to laugh at it not like the author, but to laugh, none the less. For Pierre Frondaie, who was standing behind me at the first performance, laughed with all his might. He was astonished that I applauded, thinking I did it *à rebours,* ironically. "Really," he said, between two gales, delighted by the fact that no one knew of his collaboration and the good joke he was playing on the *Raymond Rousselites,* "really, are you serious?" And he choked when I affirmed that I was not laughing, promising himself, moreover, to laugh long and laugh last, or if the wind changed, and that sometimes occurs, to claim his share of honours, later on.

The curtain had just fallen after the first act. All the critics, or nearly all, were hostile. A bird-house, it was, a cattle-shed! "You disgrace yourself, Signoret!" they cried, and that was enough to make the whole troupe, attacked through its star, weaken and give way.

No matter! The curtain rose again and there appeared two symbolic characters: The Young Poet, poor and romantic, and Fortune.

Pantomime: The Young Poet reads his verse, Fortune runs away, laughing. The Young Poet stabs himself, Fortune reappears and covers the corpse of the unfortunate youth with gold. Immediately the unappreciated inventor, Cantarel, the taciturn genius of this solitary place, enters. He muses an instant upon the Young Poet's tragic fate and cries bitterly:

— "Ah! if I were poor I would be a genius! But I am rich."

Then, recovering himself, he announces in the voice of an automaton: *"Mechanical Ballet",* and we watch the allegorical dances of Fame and Death.

Raymond Roussel, as I said before, insisted that Signoret accentuate certain speeches. He insisted especially, that he shout the one I have just quoted. Doubtless it constitutes the key to the problem and if Raymond Roussel would permit us to question him concerning it, perhaps it would enable us to pierce the peculiar mystery of his work, to divine the hidden causes of his legendary life and to understand the humour which compels him, intermittently, to manifest himself on the stage and to the public. But Raymond Roussel never replies diectly to the questions asked him.[1]

[He is thought of as a misanthrope. "He keeps himself away from the coteries and in-crowds." Nobody knows how he spends his time. I have been told he spends whole afternoons in his study pacing up and down, stopping at the closed window, drumming on the window pane, and pacing on and on till dark.

Does he go out at night? He is said to.

It is almost impossible to meet him. He employs a secretary to pass himself off as him. If one tries to telephone one gets no answer, he has managed to arrange that he can only make calls and never receive them.

I decided after the show to see him at all costs. With a couple of friends we force our way in. Is that him, this man with the teeth?]

Monsieur Raymond Roussel?

Yes.

A moment of surprise. We stammer excuses, our admiration, etc...

"Yes," he says. "There's a row, isn't there? We must cut it a bit and it will go alright."

That was all. The next day they cut it. During the *Sub-marine Ballet* strange glass floaters were supposed to bob up and down: statues, funeral wreaths, a colossal "legion of honour." In spite of these evident concessions, the police closed the theatre. But two days later and from then until the 21st of November, the performances continued amid the same hullaballoo.

At the re-opening the papers printed an announcement which this time I may be permitted to attribute entirely to Raymond Roussel:

Locus Solus is resuscitated–Kind Audience!

You thought I was dead. Do you not know that I possess the secret of "resurectine"? The pen, even that of the critics, cannot kill. But, having fluttered into my machinery, it had blocked the cog-wheels; I have repaired it. It is again very much alive and animating my six tableaux.

Meanwhile I have tidied up my laboratory, put away my tarots, my emeralds; theatrical technique, too limited for the realization of my imaginings, made it necessary for me to describe them to you when you would have preferred to see them materialized on the stage. If you are curious concerning them, read the book I published under my pseudonym Raymond Roussel,[2] you will find them there, together with a thousand other amazing inventions.

Why will you not come?[3]

What did my barker promise you that I have not fulfilled? Music by Fouret? Sets by Bertin? The creations of Poiret? For them there has been nothing but praise. My evocation of Fame, my sub-marine entertainment? The only fault you found in them was that they were too short. Did you criticize Signoret, Morton, Fabre, Flateau and Galipaux? You claimed that they had disgraced themselves!!! And yet none of them appears in his under-drawers... Your children, even, may come to see me!

My inventions? My most disconcerting comparisons? Did not that first audience laugh at them? They laughed, believe me. But you, when you have read, listened to, seen a few good farces, you say, wiping away your joyful tears; "How silly I am to laugh like this!"

No, I have not decieved you. I warned you abundantly, I believe, that I was an eccentric.

You do not come to judge me; you pay to be amused. What does it matter whether I be talented, mad, genius or joker... What the h... difference does it make to you, so long as you have your fun?

I'll see you tonight, Kind Audience... Tomorrow, every night... For as long as you like.

The scornful concession to the critics, the carefully tended mystery shrouding the real personality of the author of *Locus Solus,* the conviction of the vanity of all effort (notice the future tense of: *Why will you not come?*), Roussel's arrogance toward the man he calls his *barker*, the caustic irony with which he attacks and destroys the music, the setting and a dressmaker's creations, the offense of the vaudeville actors chosen by him, who, for once, are not obliged to appear in underwear, the psychology of hysterical laughter, the original attitude taken, the recall to decency of the "boob who pays" by the author who allows himself the luxury of playing "winners-losers", the cynical invitation to sneer, finally, the challenge of a man who will hold on till the end, because he must, knowing that in the last analysis he will be judged by his expenditures, all these are elements that defy analysis, but give us, nevertheless, the sense of that "moral lesson" pointed out by Roussel before the first roll of the drum.

★

I recalled these deductions, for which you might blame me, accusing me of trying to find, at any cost, a definite concatenation for an author—as though so many negative characteristics were not the proof of his absolute independence—two years later on my way to the rendez-vous that Raymond Roussel had at last decided to accord me.

I armed myself in advance, as much as possible, against the courteous and enigmatic surface which I foresaw he would present to me, apprehending the interview all the more, because the place named for our meeting was not his house but a woman's apartment. In any case I was sure—I had been warned—that I must content myself with a conversation devoid of the slightest confidence, save a few signs which I might interpret, after reflecting thereon, and unite to the moral idea that I had formed of Roussel through his work.

However, as I neared the Champs Elysées, I was obsessed by an image, like a detail from a dream. I said that I had been struck at our first interview by Raymond Roussel's marvellous set of teeth, and I could not help associating with these remarkable teeth the singular preoccupation of Roussel, who had had made specially, by a manifacturer of precise instruments, a little fork in platinum which Canterel used in the theatre to extract teeth by some electro-magnetic process. And the author's only contribution to the *mise en scène* of *Locus Solus* had been this extraordinary and useless jewel.

Did Roussel expect a miracle and that his utopian invention having been perfectly executed, Morton's molar would jump from the red plaque to the blue? It is unlikely. In any case, this valuable hyphen of mystery led me back to a conversation I had had in the afternoon, upon this very subject—the Roussel enigma. We had said that in every age an individual appeared rep-resenting a certain experimental spirit, directed sometimes against money, sometimes against love, sometimes against life—perhaps today against nothing; and that, if Gilles de Rais, the Marquis de Sade, Arthur Rimbaud, for example, were the chiefs of this perpetual and disturbing army of crime, Raymond Roussel, inhibited from cruelty by the actual state of society and from imagination by positivism, might well trust himself to dreams where the one and the other would appear in modern equipment, the first borrowing its elements of torture, the second its machines, from abused science.

★

I had arrived at this point in my reverie, when Raymond Roussel himself, opened the door to me. I noticed my latest book in evidence—it is the custom —on a corner of the mantlepiece, but placed in such a way that I could not see whether the leaves had been cut. When I was seated, Roussel said to me without preamble;

"It is very good. Really, we read the *Goût de Sang* with great pleasure. We were re-reading it, just now."

At this moment the disturbing statement of Canterel came into my mind.

"Well I, in a better world, would willingly eat man."

Naturally I would not mention it, had not this sudden thought been directly in line with my meditation on the stair-case. The various preoccupations which had till then accompanied me seemed to me to be akin and I was not displeased that with a word about my book Roussel had declared himself to be their father. I did not, however, see fit to dwell upon this coincidence and I took care not to reveal it. I perceived by what followed that my reserve had been justified. I would have been favoured with a smiling "It is curious, indeed," and I would have been none the wiser. I prefer to set it down here.

[I decided to talk straight away about the precocious legend surrounding him and those close to him, and tell the following anecdotes, which the reader is welcome to criticize for their exaggeration, but not for lack of spirit.

Once when Madame Roussel, the author's mother, had sent out invitations, dinner was served at the precise time on the appointed day. The guests then retired to the drawing room, whereupon a beautiful woman dressed in black walked down the monumental staircase with a book in her hand, and sat down. Till late in the night she read alous from *Les Trois Mousquetaires*.

Around the time of the performance of *Locus Solus*, Madame Roussel decided to visit India, bought a yacht, and embarked. The voyage was pleasant and the boat was about to reach port when the rich traveller called for a telescope: "So that is India!" she cried. "Captain, we are returning to France!"[4]

Was it not from India that Raymond Roussel sent an electric heater to a friend who had asked for something *rare* as a souvenir?]

He wears his ties, linen, and socks only once and then gives them to his servants—Caprice or superstition? But why should he engage a man only to polish a doorknob? The attendant must see that no mark, no mist ever dims its lustre.

"That story is apocryphal," Roussel said with a silent laugh.

"You were in the war, were you not? I asked him. An echo in the *Carnet de la Semaine...*"

"The anecdote was true, but it was wrongly told. When I made a trip around the world I went alone. Someone expressed surprise that I should do so.[5] I replied that I would have plenty of leisure to make acquaintances en route and I added; 'Was I not alone when I left for the war? I have never seen so many people!'

"Yes, I was in the war. I was at Châlons (he smiled) where I drove an automobile. We were heavily bombarded. Curious thing about bombardments, isn't it? Very curious. For example, could you tell me why Rheims which was the most bombarded town has the largest cellars in the world?"

Raymond Roussel confided to me that he does not attach much importance to his early works; *La Doublure* (1897), *Chiquenade* (1900), *La Vue* (1904).

Here is the preface to *La Doublure*.

NOTICE

As this book is a novel it must be begun at the first page and finished at the last one.

THE AUTHOR.

This book is indeed a novel. A novel of 318 pages entirely written in alexandrines. A synopsis is short and easy to make: the actor, Gaspard, elopes with Roberte, a kept woman. They take part in the carnival of Nice. Gaspard, after the trip, is deserted and stranded in a traveling theatre. This summary plot is merely a pretext for descriptions of a terrific accuracy; the end of a play, the undressing of Roberte, the carnival, a nocturnal walk, fireworks, the fair at Neuilly, etc.

Here is a passage from the *"Déshabillé"*;

Beneath one can see a sort of coarse silk double blouse
With a tight row of buttons down the middle
Like a deep black corset cover whose place it takes.
Roberte puts her hands to the top to undo it;
But Gaspard gently removes them, he prefers
To unbutton it himself; while he is at the top,
She sets to as well from the bottom, and soon
Once the two sides are open over the belly,
Their hands as they move along meet at the centre
Of the row of buttons, still closed, the top of which
He has opened meanwhile; he now insists

On undoing the last three buttons; then he opens
The two sides completely, and so uncovers
The sky blue satin of her corset; then he draws
Apart the shirt, which is gathered with a thin blue lace,
Forming a large bow in the middle...

As for the Carnival of Nice, it takes up not less than three quarters of the volume.

The conscientous reader who would like to find the key to *La Doublure* should read *Chiquenade*. He will discover there, in hermetic and symbolic form, a few of the secrets which remain the essential springs of Raymond Roussel's work. He will see in various disguises all the episodes of *La Doublure*: Panache, Fusée, Crinière, Foire, etc... He will hear Mephisto's challenge.

Who is the senseless man who fools himself
That he can pierce the scarlet cloth
With which I am clad from head to foot?

He will watch humour at work behind Chiquenade's mask and will understand how poetry destroys itself through the figure of the moths sown in the flannel which destroyed the trousers supposed to be invulnerable, in short, how *"les vers de la doublure dans la pièce du fort pantalon rouge"* symbolize *"les vers de la doublure dans la pièce* (de théâtre) *du Forban talon rouge!"*[6] And while *Chiquenade* shakes with mirth, pointing her finger at the cloud of destructive little insects, the reader will hold his sides before a hetacomb of alexandrines, but *internally*, if that can be said, like Roussel.

★

I had heard that Raymond Roussel went every evening to see *Le Bossu* while it was being played at the *Porte Saint Martin*. When I asked him the reason, I was not surprised to hear that, far from being interested in the play, he only concentrated on observing the deviations in the *mis-en-scène*, verifying the order of entrance of the supers, scrutinizing the actor's gestures, their intonations, the arrangement of the scenery, the fall of the curtain, in short, everything that can vary within the limits of the author's directions, everything indeterminate, fluctuating and not invested with that inevitable character so clearly produced by the final copy of a motion-picture film.

This concern for accuracy is the basis of all Roussel's preoccupations.

In *La Vue* the poet rejects the useless intrigue of *La Doublure* and frankly gives us descriptions of a panoramic pen-holder, a letter-head, the label on a bottle of mineral water.[7]

In a world where the essential condition of progress dwells in the perpetual passage from observation to experimentation, one is not surprised to see the author of *La Doublure* and *La Vue* become the author of *Impressions d'Afrique, Locus Solus, l'Étoile au Front,* and *Poussière de Soleils.*

There is nothing more futile than a description without an object, nothing more futile, too, than ineffective invention. Yet Roussel's later works consist exclusively of the descriptions and exploitation of incredible discoveries and inventions, interpreted with a humour definitively emancipated from laughter, and protected by a moral immunity which we must consent to recognize, some day.

Paul Valéry pointed out this invasive horology: the precision of the time, place and activity of men; and that there is less and less variation in machinery, that our lights no longer flicker and that imagination is doomed, if it does not conform, to be crushed by the machine.

Raymond Roussel has used this modern precision and established logic to construct fabulous apparatuses destined for the trans-shipment of the raw material of poetry. His work is a factory which transforms furniture into forests, explosives into pastures, newspapers into crimes. Not that the old machine turns the wrong way, but it is another one built, piece by piece, with the remotest metals, the rarest motors of such unfailing accuracy that the vocabulary is forced to give way before the charge of barbarism.

In the modern factory Raymond Roussel organizes a sort of 'work to rule'. He applies all the regulations with implacable and cruel punctiliousness. Nothing is left to accident or to chance, everything is limited, assembled, but without the least play, without oil at the joints, with no safety valves, and he congratulates himself when the wheels jam, the bars break like glass or the boilers explode. It is at this point that the dream lays before the machine those "rails of calves' lights", constructs bellows of human lungs and emprisons the ascending force of eagles in the pistons. In short, to paraphrase the well-known verse, one may say that Roussel lives in a world where dream is the brother of action.

Absolute precision proves itself to be destructive, it is the new form of humour—that of Raymond Roussel.

It is rare not to find in an author's life as well as in his dreams the manifest equivalent of his intellectual or spiritual preoccupations. You will not be surprised that Raymond Roussel should have a taste for firearms:

"It is significant," says one critic, "that Raymond Roussel is fond of sport in his spare time. A crack shot with the pistol, he has no less than forty-five medals and he won the Gastinne-Rennette gold medal in 1909."

"We must be absolutely modern," said Rimbaud. That is to be the sum of all the past, of all the present and also of Σ; Σ, mystery, Σ which permits us to abolish the limitation of time, Σ that confers upon the machines imagined by Roussel the eternal character that defies death; for beside them, in ten years, those constructed by the industrialism of our age will be nothing but old carcasses.

It appealed to Raymond Roussel's sense of humour to acquire one of these old carcasses. It was an old but very luxurious automobile, carefully kept, very shining and hence all the more phantomlike. People attributed it to his habitual eccentricity. I personally imagine that Roussel voluntarily retreated from Σ on this side of progress, that is to say, he wished to live in an epoch, still quite our own, but with that slight distance, which instead of enhancing one's prestige, infinitely diminished it. If he had travelled in a coach-and-four, people would have accused him of masquerading; seeing him in a "jalopy" they were simply scandalised.

This experiment having been successful, he had only to try its antithesis and to go beyond Σ in time. So he ordered a splendid automobile-house, marvellously furnished, decorated with precious woods and comprising a dining-room that could be transformed into a studio, a bedroom, a bathroom with W.C. and a room for the chauffeur. He then undertook several voyages. Need I say that he aroused the same curiosity and scandal everywhere?

"It is very agreeable," he confided to me. "I stop where I please and go on when I please, a regular land yacht. And I am alone."

"Alone?" I said, "But people..."

"Yes, that's true, but one can avoid the villages. Mussolini, whom I went to see in Rome, made the same remark. I replied that he did not need such an automobile to attract the attention of the crowd. Ah! the pope too, wished to see my auto. But as he cannot leave the Vatican and I could not decently —I wonder why—drive my *roulotte* in there, he sent someone, the nuncio, who went away filled with admiration."

[Without ever betraying this anonymous grandness, Roussel tried every possible way to get people interested in his stories. The stage shows of *Impressions d'Afrique* were merely curtain raisers put on in Paris and the provinces in which he did not hesitate to take a walk-on role so as to enjoy the effect. *Locus Solus* derived its effect from the music halls. In *L'Étoile au front* Roussel renounced theatrical accessories or at least reduced them to a minimum—a few objects placed in a living room where they provided an excuse for new developments in the course of five acts. This flop induced him to use another approach: magic enchantment. He used this in *Poussière de Soleils* but as unsuccessfully as ever. Was Roussel sincere, and did he wish to seem so? Did he expect to receive recognition in the end? I cannot believe so when I realise that the outrageously made-up young sailor in *Impressions d' Afrique* accepted a present of baked apples without demur, and that at the first few evenings of *L'Étoile au front* he was very concerned to know whether two hundred small benches had been set out in the Upper Circle of the Vaudeville as he had asked.

Besides that, in the quotes that he always added to the programmes of his stage shows, or to the books he published, I can only really see a collection of jokes set out in an order that is not irrelevant, and constituting a sort of preface in which criticism quite simply loses its right to exist. With Marcel Proust and Edmond Rostand at the head of the list beside Claude Balleroy, Signoret, Regine Flory, Royaumont, it is an excellent joke to follow that with a jumbled heap of quotes from the story-tellers of Marrakesh, the Gulf Stream, the Child-Hero, Hoffmann, Stevenson, cinema, encyclopaedias, Calif Omar, tropical ideas, the Lives of the Saints, demonology, the planetary system, the magic of words, Shakespeare, Lucien Godin and Armand Massard, Einstein, Victor Hugo, madness, Henry Bidou, Alfred Jarry, Apollinaire, Lautreamont, Rimbaud, Gounod and Alphonse Daudet.

There could hardly be a better way of putting critics on trial and I would bet that Raymond Roussel in spite of his courtesy, has thought of assembling all these messy items into a new book.]

What surprises does this Marcel Proust of the dream still hold in store for us, and how far will he drive his silent pack of steam-shovels? By what means will he try to touch us and what elephant-trainer will he choose to present his freak?

He confessed to me that he was tired of his experiments. But who can make a *chess player* despair? No doubt the machine will again be exhibited, somewhere.[8] We will verify the inflexible laws governing its operation, it will be proved to us once more, not with a candle, but with powerful projectors, that no one is hiding in the the cupboards or drawers of the automaton, and Raymond Roussel, in the carcass of the Turk, will lose this new match against the public, but he will always win against himself.

_1928

Notes

1. When the translation of this essay was published in *Transition* in March 1928, one month after its original publication, several sections had been cut "at the request of M. Raymond Roussel, himself". These cuts have been restored here and are indicated by square brackets. They are translated by Antony Melville, the literal translations of the poetry in this essay are also his.
2. "Raymond Roussel" was, of course, not a pseudonym, which makes this statement rather puzzling. However Caradec, in his biography of Roussel, attributes the whole of this 'announcement' to Pierre Frondaie, rather than Roussel, which may explain the error.
3. Apparently Vitrac either misread this sentence, or transcribed a copy of it which contained a misprint. In all other versions of this text discovered by Jean Ferry this sentence is in the past tense.
4. As Ferry points out in his introduction to this article in *Bizarre*, this anecdote was normally associated with Roussel himself, rather than his mother.
5. Mussolini!
6. In English: "The worms in the lining of the patch of the heavy red trousers" and "the lines of verse of the understudy in the play of Red-Heel the Buccaneer."
7. You will read with interest the article devoted to Roussel by Robert de Montesquiou in his book *Elus et Appelés*, under the title "A Difficult Author":
   "These verses apply themselves as might an entomologist studying the habits of insects, to describing what they discover in the immense captive seascape of the minute sphere; and it is here that Roussel's art of splitting hairs, not into four, as the saying goes, but into four hundred and forty thousand, to start with, appears to me as a phenomenon worthy of being pointed out to those who delight in analysis, enumeration and nomenclature. [Author's note]
8. The last paragraph refers to the illustration beside the epigraph from *Le Merle Blanc*, a periodical of the period. This represents the automatic chess-player exposed as fraudulent by Edgar Poe (the essay was translated by Baudelaire). Also, *echec* has the double meaning of "chess" or "failure". Five years after this article was published, Roussel took up chess and invented, within a short while, a new formula for the knight/bishop checkmate which aroused some interest within chess circles.

SALVADOR DALI

Raymond Roussel: "Nouvelles Impressions d'Afrique"

Translation   Martin Sorrell

Of all the books of our time, this one is the most "poetically elusive", and thus the one which will endure the longest. A sublimely disparaging use of metaphor situates this writing on the borderland of mental deficiency. Roussel's analogies are the product of the most direct, unmediated associations, quite anecdotal and random. They allow us to witness the darkest and deepest conflicts anyone has ever lived through. Indeed we must look on the sequence of "compound elements" as *relations*, since they unfold in a coherent, consecutive way, and remorselessly present a number of very clear, obsessive invariables; for example, fried eggs, multiple allusions to the smell of urine after the ingestion of asparagus, etc. The irrational nature of Roussel's book is established beyond doubt by its universe of relationships between elements. How far these relationships are objective can be ascertained experimentally. It is in the systematic, unlimited use of this mechanism of incontrovertible, microscopic associations—a mechanism intended to "give status" to a content which is feverish and obsessive in its choice of compound elements—that *Nouvelles Impressions d'Afrique* reveals itself to us as the dream journey of the new paranoiac phenomena.

The choice of illustrations confirms once again the genius of Raymond Roussel.

—1933

Mortal Interlude

RAYMOND ROUSSEL LEFT PARIS ON THE 31ST. OF MAY, 1933* FOR PALERMO, HAVING ARRANGED FOR THE POSTHUMOUS PUBLICATION OF *Comment j'ai ecrit certains de mes livres*, THE REMAINING ESSAYS IN THIS ANTHOLOGY WERE WRITTEN IN THE LIGHT OF ITS REVELATIONS. ROUSSEL DIED IN PALERMO ON THE NIGHT OF THE 13TH. AND 14TH. OF JULY.

It is not known whether or not he had seen Dali's review of Nouvelles Impressions d'Afrique *before his departure.*

ANDRÉ BRETON
Raymond Roussel

Translation

Martin Sorrell

The difficulty which exists in distinguishing, at a certain distance, between an authentic automaton and a false one has been the object of the greatest curiosity down the centuries. From Albert the Great's android porter who ushered in guests with a few words, down to the chess player made famous by Poe, by way of Jan Müeller's iron fly which flew about and then alighted on his hand, by way of Vaucanson's famous duck, not forgetting the homunculi from Paracelsus to Achim von Arnim, the most moving, ambiguous relationship between animal life, especially human, and its mechanical simulacram has existed. The specifically modern way of dealing with this ambiguity has been to transpose the automaton from the exterior to the interior world, letting it freely develop in the mind itself. For psycho-analysis has discerned, in the recesses of the mental store-house, the presence of an anonymous mannequin, "without eyes, without nose, without ears", closely resembling those painted by Chirico around 1916. This mannequin, cleaned of the spiders' webs which hid it from view and paralysed it, has shown that it is extremely mobile, "superhuman" (it is out of the very need to give full licence to this mobility that surrealism was born). This unusual being, free from the monstrous deformities which disfigure Mary Shelley's admirable *Frankenstein*, enjoys the ability to move about without the least friction, through time as through space, and in a single stride it leaps the un-bridgeable gap which supposedly separates action from dream. The marvellous thing is that this automaton should dwell in us all, ready to be released. All it needs is a little help to recapture, as did Rimbaud, the sense of its absolute innocence and power.

It is well-known that "pure psychic automatism", in the current inter-pretation of that phrase, means only a boundary-state which would require of human beings that they relinquish entirely the moral and logical control of their actions. Without agreeing to go so far, or rather to stay fixed in that position, it happens that from a certain point onwards, they find themselves governed by a motor of unheard-of force, they obey in a mathematical way an apparently cosmic impulse which cannot be understood. The question which arises in respect of these automata, as of others, is whether there is hidden in them a *conscious* being. And *to what extent conscious?* we may ask when confronted with Roussel's writing. Admittedly, during his lifetime, a few people had clearly sensed that he owed his prodigious gift of invention to a technique he had himself discovered, that he was making use, as it were, of a crib for the imagination, like a crib for the memory. This method was divulged after his death in his work entitled *Comment j'ai écrit certains de mes livres*. We know now that the method consisted of composing with homonymic or more or less homophonic words, two sentences with utterly different meanings, and of making these sentences the key points at the beginning and end of his story. The story-building element should develop from the first to the second by means of a different activity in which each "double entendre" of these two outer sentences is linked to another "double entendre" by the preposition 'to' (*à*). According to Roussel himself, "the particular characteristic of this method was that it brought about a number of *factual equations* which it then became necessary to solve logically". It was a matter of dissipating, making disappear the greatest illogicality in a literary subject by a series of passes through which the rational constantly restricts and tempers the irrational.

Roussel, along with Lautreamont, is the greatest hypnotist of modern times. In Roussel, the conscious person is extremely painstaking. ("Each sentence costs me blood". He tells Leiris that each line of *Nouvelles Impressions d'Afrique* has demanded fifteen hours or so of work). The conscious part of the self grapples ceaselessly with the highly authoritarian unconscious. (It is fairly symptomatic that he should have remained faithful to a philosophically untenable technique for nearly forty years without seeking to modify it or replace it with another). Roussel's humour, deliberate or not, lies entirely in this interplay of disproportionate balances. Jean Lévy[1] writes, "there are a few of us who have heard in Roussel's work the lugubrious tick-tock of the infernal machine which Lautreamont deposited at the gateway of the mind, and we have greeted with admiration each of its liberating explosions".

The same critic has rightly observed that, in this work, a proper account has yet to be given of humour, of obsession and of repression. Roussel indeed had a brush with psycho-pathology, his case having even provided Dr. Pierre Janet the opportunity to publish a paper entitled *The Psychological Characteristics of Ecstacy*. His suicide (if suicide it was) confirms the idea that throughout his literary career, he remained an abnormal person. At nineteen, when he was finishing his poem *La Doublure*, he experienced Nietzsche's ultimate ecstasy. "One feels that a particular piece one is working on is a masterpiece, that one is a genius... I was the equal of Shakespeare or Dante, I felt what the 70 year-old Hugo felt, what Napoleon felt in 1811, what Tannhauser dreamt at the Venusberg. What I was writing was wreathed in light, I closed the curtains for I was afraid that the slightest chink might let escape the luminous rays which emanated from my pen, I wanted to pull back the screen suddenly and flood the world with light. If I had left these sheets of paper lying about, shafts of light would have been created and would have travelled as far as China, and the demented crowd would have burst into the house".

As far as China... This child who adored Jules Verne, this great lover of *guignol*, this very wealthy man who had built for his travels the most luxurious self-propelled caravan in the world remained to his end the worst denigrator, the most negative critic of real journeys. Leiris says that "in Pekin, Roussel shut himself away after the most cursory visit of the city", just as he stayed in the cabin of his ship, writing, when he had the opportunity of going ashore in Tahiti.

The marvellous originality of Roussel is that he rejects in a far-sighted and deeply significant way old-fashioned, simplistic realism, whether or not it terms itself "socialist". He offers an affront to which there is no reply. "Martial", as the author of *Locus Solus* is called in Pierre Janet's paper, "has a very interesting conception of literary beauty. The work must contain nothing which is real, no observations about the world, nothing intellectual, but only compositions of a totally imaginary sort; these are in themselves ideas of a non-human world."

—1933

Notes

1. Jean Lévy is Jean Ferry's real name. The article quoted here is presumably his "Raymond Roussel", published in *Documents 34*, 9 & 10, 1934, which was signed with this name.

Michel Butor
The Methods of Raymond Roussel

Translation   Roderick Masterton

Anyone who was enchanted by the magical *Impressions d'Afrique* may well be sadly disappointed on first reading *Comment j'ai écrit certains de mes livres.*

Roussel tells us: "I chose two almost identical words. For example, *billard* (billiard table) and *pillard* (plunderer). To these I added similar words capable of two different meanings, and thus I obtained two almost identical sentences . . .

The two phrases found, it was a case of writing a story which could begin with the first and end with the second.

Now it was from the resolution of this problem that I derived all my material.

. . . Expanding this method, I began to search for new words related to *billard* always giving them a meaning other than that which first came to mind, and each time this provided me with further creation . . .

As the method developed, I was led to take a phrase from which I drew images by distorting it, a little as though it were a case of deriving them from the drawings of a rebus."[1]

But, you object, this dream is then merely the product of an ingenious machine operating in a void? In that case, it can have nothing to say. It amounts only to a curious, amusing and transitory arabesque, like fleeting reflections in water. It is pointless looking for any inherent aim or meaning.

Clearly, Roussel would have been the first to protest against such an interpretation. His method of creation, he says, is essentially poetic. Indeed it is a process based on an extraordinarily developed, not to say, exploded rhyme.

He has given us a very clear demonstration of his method in one of those stories which serve as themes for the tableaux presented by the "Theatre of the Incomparables". It is *Handel composing the Vesper Oratorio*. In the course of a conversation with his friend Lord Corfield, Handel, now old and blind, says that he is confident he could write an entire oratorio, sufficiently substantial to take its palce in his complete works, "even on a theme mechanically constructed using a purely random method."

To prove his case, the composer takes seven holly branches to which he attaches seven ribbons, corresponding to the colours of the rainbow, and each one corresponding to a note on the scale. Identifying them by touch alone, he selects one for each of the twenty-three steps of the great staircase he is descending, and on the bannister inscribes with a pen the note thus revealed.

"In his hands, the weirdly-shped theme assumed a beautiful and interesting form, due to ingenious combinations of harmony and rhythm. The same phrase of twenty-three notes recurred throughout, each time differently presented, and alone constituted the famous Vesper oratorio, a work of unmistakable power and serenity, still universally admired."

Roussel tells us about the technical origins of this story, that is, his search for a phonetic equivalent for Hugo's line *"Une vase rempli du vin de l'espérence"* (A jug full of the wine of hope). Unfortunately he can only remember part of his initial phrase: *"... sept houx rampe lit ... Vesper"* (seven hollies balustrade read ... Vesper). From this alone, we can see the extent of the phonetic difference between these two sequences of words, and we can also see that it is quite possible to find other equivalents, equally plausible, which could be used to construct very different stories.

As Handel composed the Vesper oratorio around a single phrase, so under extreme circumstances Roussel might have been able to write a whole book using just one phrase from Hugo. But, as he tells us himself, the mere working-out of these equivalences took an enormous amount of time. On occasions, he needed a whole day to arrive at a single homonym.

Obviously he was not satisfied until his solution seemed to open up onto something else. Some deep, unsuspected purpose guided him towards the choice of certain resonances, and their elaboration allowed him to unveil imaginary landscapes which had seemed permanently prohibited by his education, his social position, his very self.

What seems henceforth to be fundamental to this method is the close attention paid to the words themselves, and the desire to investigate systematically the way in which they are used. "Always giving them meanings other than that which first came to mind."

In his aleatorally constructed sequences, in this type of hallucinatory reading which consists of asking any text at all if it can be read differently, his object is not so much to fuse words to their habitual meaning (which would be an acceptance of their exhaustion, making them vague and easily replaceable with crude synonyms) than to endow them with all their strength and wholeness. He struggles to extract the most from their tensions and their particular qualities. He makes them disclose the domains which they have allowed him to glimpse, and to which they are the key.

If we read more closely what Roussel says about the inception of

Impressions d'Afrique, we will see at first hand the way in which one by one he builds his linguistic "finds" into an edifice which only reveals itself to him little by little, and in which these "finds" progressively lose their initial appearance of arbitrariness, being in fact, systematically "encountered". There are no episodes, however ludicrous or futile they might seem at first sight, which do not have their place in the overall organisation of the book. In Roussel's great bazaar, there is a thread of meaning which we are asked to follow.

One of the most remarkable peculiarities of *Locus Solus* and of *Impressions d'Afrique* is that nearly all the scenes are described twice. First, we witness them as if they were a ceremony or a theatrical event; and then they are explained to us, by their history being recounted. This is particularily the case in *Impressions*; the author went to the trouble, after publication, of inserting a slip of green paper on which he suggested that "those readers not initiated in the art of Raymond Roussel are advised to begin this book at p. 212 and go on to p. 455, and then turn back to p. 1 and read to p. 211."

It is not the juxtaposition of words which explains the wealth of repetitions and of reproductive apparatus encountered in these texts. On the contrary, it is this obsession which makes us realise what an irresistable compulsion, and authentic and deep-seated instinct, led Roussel to choose these singular methods, and not any others, for writing these works.

The fact that Roussel's first published book, written in a state of extraordinary exaltation was entitled *La Doublure* is in itself of the greatest significance. From the crucial role played in his work by homonyms, we know quite simply that it has nothing to do with coincidence. This novel, composed in alexandrines, for the most part consists of a fastidiously detailed description of the carnival at Nice. Another book, *La Vue*, takes this insistence on the depiction of minutiae even further: several hundred lines are required to do justice to the label on a bottle of mineral water.

Between these, he had written a certain number of short stories each of which began and ended with the same sequence of words, identical apart from one letter. *Impressions d'Afrique* and *Locus Solus* are shot through with a wealth of insidious repetitions, like watermarks.

The reproduction of detail which he had experimented with in *La Doublure* and *La Vue*, and which found such a curious expression in stories such as *Chiquenaude*, is supported by the systems which fill the prodigious imaginary world into which we are led at the exact moment of its perfection. It would take too long to list all the examples. Here are just some of the more striking ones:

On the coat which Bedu the inventor's loom is weaving automatically, and which "made possible the manufacture of magical cloths similar to those of the masters", we may admire the depiction of the Flood, "and so great was the ingenuity of the fabulous cogs and gears of the machine that the result could stand comparison with the finest water-colours; the faces, with their agitated expressions, had marvellously fleshy tones, from the weather-beaten brow of the old man and the milky white of the young woman to the fresh pink of the baby; the water, employing the whole range of blues, became covered in reflecting patterns and its limpid depths changed from place to place."

Immediately after, the sculptor Fuxier offers little blue pastilles which, on melting, make pictures in the water. One is a scene of a feast, and we read that "the detail was so subtle that here and there the shadow cast by crumbs on the tablecloth could be discerned."

Then there is a firework which throws "remarkably executed" pictures, made of flames, into the the sky. Indeed, in one of them, "an impeccable horseman on a trotting mount greeted an unseen amazon as he passed by."

This is on pp. 124-140 of *Impressions d'Afrique*. If we examine their position within the book, we shall find that progressively they yield their meaning.

Broadly, the work describes a celebration of deliverance. A boat has been wrecked and all its passengers are prisoners of the cruel black king Talou who already has in his custody the young explorer Louise Montalescot and her brother Norbert. On the 25th of June, we witness one after the other the self-coronation of Talou, the execution of the condemned, and a kind of superior music-hall, "the gala of the Incomparables". When night falls, the whole population goes down to the river and the night-time activities begin with a sort of miracle: a magician restores the sight of the queen's daughter. Then we see the three demonstrations I have just quoted; when silence is restored after the explosion of rockets, a burst of thunder is heard in the sky, a prelude to three events it is worth dwelling on.

The first is the putting to death of Djizme in the huge Square of Trophies in the very heart of Ejur, capital of the empire. Dragged from her prison, she is led into the midst of the now silent crowd, and placed without resistance on a lightning-conductor bed. She takes with both hands a parchment map and contemplates it with an expression of joy and pride. Then, for the first time since her imprisonment, she catches sight of her too-ingenious lover Nair, bound to a pedestal by delicate webbing, and at the moment when once again her arms stretch out to him, a bolt of lightning fixes in an unalterable expression of tenderness her wide-open eyes which ensnare those of Nair. After this execution, the sky becomes clear again.

Then the hypnotist Darriand, who has been striving to perfect his art, tries an experiment on Seilkor, a wretched black madman. A blank wall serves as a screen on which is projected a series of images which the spectator confuses so much with reality, thanks to the exhalations of certain ocean plants placed above his head, that the sight of a hyperborean landscape immediately induces a great drop in his body temperature.

He is made to relive episodes from his childhood. "At once, some coloured film, placed in front of the lamp, cast a picture on the white screen, setting in front of Seilkor a charming little girl with fair hair, aged about twelve and extremely pretty and graceful; above the portrait were these words: 'The Young Candiot'." This vision profoundly disturbs the young man, who cries out "Nina, Nina". For no doubt the immediate cause of Seilkor's madness is a head-wound, as a result of which he can no longer recognise anything at all: but it has also rendered him powerless to deal with the root of another, older problem. Around the age of ten, he had been in love with a little girl whose death he accidentally caused. So he had fled from this girl's relatives, and from all the places where they had shared their love, taking with him as his only momento a paper costume which she had made and which he had been wearing the last time he saw her. It is these rags, now much too small for him, which he has worn without interruption since the day he was wounded.

One after the other, the episodes of their life together are brought back to the suffering young man. Seilkor "stripped by Darriand of his paper rags, suddenly looked about him like someone coming out of his sleep, and then murmured softly: 'Oh, I remember, I remember now . . . Nina . . . Tripoli . . .The Oo Valley . . .' " The unfortunate madman, beyond hope a moment ago, now recognises all the faces in his redemptive return to good health.

And it is at this point that there takes place the sensational first performance of the final scene of *Romeo and Juliet* in its restored version. Here is how Roussel concludes Shakespeare's drama:

Contrary to tradition, the hero and heroine are reunited before dying. Juliet awakes before the poison has had time to work on Romeo. "The two lovers, arm in arm, exchanged many caresses, giving themselves up to a trembling ecstacy."

Romeo adorns Juliet's neck with a string of red-hot coals which do not burn her at all; but, sensing that her lover has only a few moments to live, she drinks the rest of the phial so that she may die alongside him. Both then become the victims of hallucinations in which they witness scenes they were told about in their childhood and whose aim was to steer them into the paths of virtue.

In the text, which as one can see has been much modified, it is necessary to insert a double prologue; on the one hand, the edifying speeches of the learned monk Valdivieso to young Montague, on the other the graceful or terrible stories told to the little Capulet girl by her wet-nurse.

These apparitions all have an accusatory quality, in the middle of a scene made even more macabre by the green light of the flames which flicker behind the bed of the two lovers, Juliet seems rigid with fear, and at the moment she sees coming down towards her a second Romeo "who personifies the light and living soul of the motionless corpse stretched out beside her, and who comes to take her away to her eternal abode", she, seemingly out of her mind, turns her head away in an attitude of indifference, and falls dead beside her lifeless lover.

In finding each other, the two lovers rediscover their childhood, and it is important to note that, in *Impressions d'Afrique* they are played by two children of 7 and 8 years.

These terrifying hallucinations, which seem to be the proof that they have been condemned, punished for having transgressed the laws of the monk Valdivieso, do not stop Romeo from returning, a smile on his face, in order to take his companion off to her "eternal abode". Her death, like that of Djizme, whose smile is fixed for eternity by the lightning flash, is at the same time a transfiguration, a passing-through to the other side of the mirror, an absolute victory over the ravages of time. But why doesn't Juliet accept this omen of good fortune? Because she cannot believe that he is indeed coming back so long as she sees the corpse beside her and she maintains her fidelity to the latter in the face of something which may be just a sham. There is no doubt that she has come victoriously through this ultimate trial.

The whole scene is framed by the "note of C, quite sharp, which in all its perfection and purity, sang out clearly in the night", produced by the wheels of the Roman chariot which serves as a stage. Sound punctuations are of great importance in the structure of Roussel's texts.

Fuxier lends his help in this last scene by creating some of the effects, and once when the "C" note is silenced, he steps in a third time to offer a bunch of grapes whose seeds contain minute pictures, the result of some biological engineering on the original pip.

Roussel tells us that the subjects of certain of his vegetable sculptures spring from the re-working of the title of one of Cherbuliez's novels, *Les*

Inconséquences de M. Dommel, but we can readily understand the transition from the word "grape" to "seed",[2] taken first to mean a part of a fruit, an element of the bunch, then to denote the reproductive function, crucially fulfilled by sexuality, again an accurate, faithful image. Here is an admirable example of how an object can be constituted metaphorically on the basis of the semantic irridescense of a given word.

Fuxier's "bunch" thus underlines the close relationship between the three reproductions and the three love stories in each of which a reproductive process plays a part: Nair's web, Darriand's magic lantern, and Fuxier's second pastilles.

After this strange realisation, Fogar's grand demonstration takes place, which is very much the heart of the book, but from which I will single out just one element: the photographic plant discovered by the young man on the sea floor. At a precise moment in its growth, it fixes those images presented to it, and subsequently reproduces them indefinitely in the order in which they appeared. We can see that Fuxier's vine constitutes a sort of early sketch of this mysterious example of vegetable life. Fogar finishes his demonstration with artificial thunder that answers the real thunder clap announcing the execution of Djizme.

One attraction only is reserved for the next day, at dawn: the activation of the painting machine, now complete and ready, which Louise Montalescot has been working on for a considerable time. This machine is the most elaborate example of the process of reproduction brought to our attention in *Impressions d'Afrique*:

"The finished work, seen as a whole, gave an impression of uncommonly intense colouring and remained strictly true to the original as each person was able to confirm by a quick glance at the actual garden."

This event signals the liberation of the white prisoners who after this are all able to return to their countries of origin. After the complete re-telling of all the episodes, and their clarification by their histories, everything goes back into the narrator's memory, just as the scenes of their childhood passed before the eyes of Seilkor, or of Romeo and Juliet. "With my attention scarcely distracted by my purely mechanical task, I couldn't stop myself from thinking, in the vast silence of the morning, about the many adventures which have been crowding my life for many months."

One further detail, which only goes to reinforce this observation: the last prisoner, young Carmichael, who had incurred the king's displeasure for not being able, the day before, to sing accurately to him the unintelligible verses of the epic *The Battle of Tez*, will be released only when he has succeeded in giving a faultless rendition of it.

This theme of recitation is already present in the final pages of the book alongside the unheard recitation which accompanies Nair's web: "Looking like a living statue, he made a number of slow, punctual movements as he rapidly murmured a series of words learnt by heart ... The phrases he recited *sotto voce* had the function of punctuating and organising his risky, precise manoeuvres; the least error would cause irreversible damage to the whole programme, and without the automatic memory-aid provided by a certain formula learned word for word, Nair could never have achieved his aim." It should be noted that it is his artistry, and the faultless recitation that results from it, that ensures his life will be spared, just as it is the perfect rendition of *The Battle of Tez* which restores Carmichael his freedom.

We see that Roussel organises the episodes which he has "found" not in an arbitrary grouping but according to a metaphorical and musical development which, as it were, buoys up its meaning and authority. The fundamental theme which underlies all this celebration, is that of salvation, of healing, of liberation achieved through the precise repetition of something; music is the supreme expression of that repetition, transposed into language by versification, particularily by the repetition of sounds in rhyme, and ultimately by rhyme taken to its limits, synonymous with the embodiment of this method of invention.

If we now look at *Locus Solus,* we will find new variations on this theme. After having shown his guests the immense glass cage in which eight corpses re-enact at will the decisive moment of their lives under the tireless and wide-eyed gaze of their relatives standing up against the wall, Dr. Canterel takes them to a pavilion where he has placed the unfortunate Lucius Egroizard, an artist and scholar of genius, driven mad by the appalling death of his daughter Gilette. Using means so strange that it is impossible to describe them in fewer words than Roussel himself, he goes over endlessly the circumstances of her murder. He cannot resign himself to her death as his unstinting efforts to make a child's layette demonstrate.

At the moment when he appears to notice for the first time the visitors who are bringing his doctor to him, he utters the simple command "sing". Now, amongst them there is the singer Malvina, who with good grace, performs the opening of the confidante's aria in *Abimélech*, a "recent biblical opera". After the first phrase, "O Rebecca", her strange one-man audience asks her to stop and begin again. By means which, predictably, are unusual in the extreme, he records the voice in which he thinks he has heard echoes of the mumblings of his daughter, and then systematically he deforms the voice, like an electronic musician. At last, "from the very depths of the horn there emerged, on the vowel 'a', a long happy syllable which, reminiscent of the stumblings of young children eager to learn how to speak, bore a strong resemblance to the model provided by the end of the motif: 'O Rebecca'. He cries out at that point, 'Her voice . . . it's my daughter's voice . . . It's you, my little Gilette, they haven't killed you'."

"And, amongst these unfinished phrases, the beginnings of a word, endlessly spoken, came like an answering echo." From this point on there is a rapid progress in Egroizard's recovery.

The following two chapters describe scenes and apparatus which offer close structural similarities with Fogar's demonstration. But I want to turn straight-away to the very end of the book, which emphasises the importance of the chapter we have just examined. The day before leaving *Locus Solus*, the guests watch some metallic lacework being weaved from a roll which happens to be the last of its kind; the weaver hasn't the remotest idea how to make more. The sacrifice of this precious material gives a special quality to this day, and makes it stand out from all the rest.

Now, the corpses in their glass cages are indestructible, and as often as one wishes one can supply them with the necessary bits and pieces for a repetition of their supreme moment; the mosaic of teeth made by the aerial paviour continues, and its completion is consigned by Roussel to a deliberately vague future etc . . . The only event which really occurs that day is the curing of Lucius Egroizard by Malvina's song.

The episodes of these two books, one can readily see, are connected in a figurative elucidation; linked to certain fundamental themes, they constitute a network of parables which throw light one on the other. Thus, from the indeterminate repetition of final moments acted out inside their glass cages by the corpses, we move, in Lucius Egroizard's story, to repetition as final moment, deliverance at one and the same time both from death and from these vain returns, perpetual yet perpetually imperfect.

One of the most beautiful passages in *Impressions d'Afrique* gives us a way of interpreting this rapport very precisely. We are referring to the legend of the Bewitched of Lake Ontario, the final episode of which becomes the subject of one of the *tableaux vivants* executed by Soreau during the Incomparables' Gala.

Young Ursula is detested by her mother-in-law who, with the help of her sister and two brothers, seeks to get rid of her by drowning her in the lake. Her old and faithful servant Maffa, outraged by this plan, goes to see Nô the magician to inform him of what is happening and to get his help. At the moment when the conspirators are "about to toss the body of Ursula into the waves", he begins a terrible incantation which brings about a four-fold metamorphosis:

Gervaise, the cruel mother-in-law, is turned into a she-ass, unable to move, rooted in front of a trough full of bran which she is unable to eat, her jaw held shut by means of a seton, unable to flee, a golden portcullis descending each time to block her way, whichever direction she tries to take,

her sister, Agatha, is turned into a goose, running wildly in all directions, chased by the north wind,

one of the brothers has his head transformed into that of a boar, and he shoots off, straight as an arrow, in hot pursuit of an egg, a glove and a wisp of straw which, despite his best efforts, will not stop bobbing and jumping in his hands,

the other brother, is thrown into the lake and begins to swim round and round and round, changed into a pike.

Ursula then asks the magician if there might not be some way of freeing these poor wretches who in her opinion do not deserve this eternal punishment. Nô answers that once a year, on the anniversary of their bewitching, their four trajectories will coincide. "This meeting will last only a brief second, for no moment of rest is to be allowed the unfortunate runaways. If, during this scarcely perceptible instant, a kindly hand were to use any kind of device, whatever it might be, to fish the pike out of the water and land it on the bank, the spell will immediately be broken and the four victims will revert to their human form. But the slightest clumsiness in this delicate manoeuvre will risk setting back the opportunity of making another attempt until the next year."

So, a year later, all the protagonists are gathered once more, and the girl, net in hand, attempts the rescue operation. "But the mesh, although fine and strong, allows the prisoner to escape; he falls back into the water, and continues his mad circuits.

The juggler and the goose, momentarily re-united with the she-ass, crossed paths without slowing down, and very quickly disappeared in opposite directions.

Everything seems to indicate that Ursula's setback was due to a supernatural influence, for, after it had happened, it was clear that there was no tear in the net, which remained in perfect order."

It was only at the fifth attempt that she was able "deftly and swiftly to land the pike high up on the bank without giving it the chance to slip through the ensnaring web." Immediately, the spell was broken, and the four unhappy people resumed their human form.

It is superfluous to stress the fact that we are dealing here with the theme of the great cycle of the year, the eternal return. What is all the more remarkable is the way in which the notion of imitation is brought out. Each year the event tries to conform to the ideal model put forward by the magician, and each time it fails. What is reproduced in a natural fashion is a perpetual failure; the event is mapped out and dissolves before really having taken place. This is also what occurs in the glass cage where each of the decisive events which are reiterated at will are in effect decisive failures, which lead to death. And it is not possible to get past this; the event only truly has reality to the extent that it includes what Kierkegaard called a repetition, to the extent that the second instance includes an absolute awareness of the preceding one; then this event which always fails, which always vanishes at the very moment when one thought it was in fact happening, becomes solid, a secure base from which one can make definitive changes. The amelioration of the world becomes a realisable aim; lead changes into gold. This is what validates the comparison Breton has made between Roussel's adventure and the Philospher's stone.

All of Roussel's writing then, like Proust's, is a search for lost time, but this recovery of childhood is in no sense a retrogressive movement; rather it is, if you will allow me the expression, a return into the future, for the event rediscovered changes its level and meaning.

Too little is known about this man's life, but there is one extant document of considerable importance. It is the article which Pierre Janet devoted to him in *De l'Angoisse á l'Extase,* and which in particular provides us with details about the crisis which the author lived through around the age of twenty.

" 'I knew glory,' he said, '. . . what I wrote was bathed in rays of light, I closed the curtains as I was afraid of the merest chink which might have allowed to escape from my room the luminous shafts which flooded from my pen; I wanted to withdraw the screen suddenly and illuminate the world. To have left these papers lying around would have created streams of light which would have travelled as far as China, and the delirious crowd would have come crashing down on my house. But my precautions were useless, rays of light flowed out of me, penetrated the walls, I carried the sun within me and could not prevent this tremendous fulguration of myself . . .' "

Janet notes that Roussel, or Martial as he calls him, "retained a burning wish, a wild desire to experience this feeling again, if only for five minutes." " 'Ah,' he says, 'that sensation of moral sun, I've never been able to rediscover it. I'm looking for it, and I always shall. I'd willingly exchange all my remaining years for one moment of that glory'."

His work abounds in representations of that glory, in particular the metaphor of gold in all its forms. This effort towards literary glory which at first seems so vain and puerile was in fact nothing other than a means of winning back that which his ecstasy had allowed him to sense, to win it back once and for all, and it is thus not only Roussel's whole work but also his whole life which unfolds beneath the sign of an active repetition.

We can see that the methods he tells us about in *Comment...* are closely linked to his themes, that they constitute one of its elements. To conclude, let us re-read a few lines of *L'Étoile au Front*:

" 'Did he sniff out cryptograms?'

'. . . and intensified his attention. Soon, words, one to a line, traced a kind of thick, imperfect diagonal down the sheet of paper.'

'It remained to fill the page with the phrases which provided their correct asylum.'

'A long and awkward task . . .'

'The primitive words written at a slant indeed concerned the vanished gems . . .' "

—1950

Notes

1   As translated by Trevor Winkfield. [Trans. note]

2. Roussel's distortion of *"Les Inconséquences de Monsieur Dommel"* is *"Raisin qu'un Celte hante démon scie Eude Rome elle"* [Grape that a Celt haunts devil saw Odo Rome she].

JEAN FERRY
Raymond Roussel in Paradise

Translation   Paul Hammond

When Raymond Roussel arrived after death in his rightful country, but where at first he could not get his bearings, Jules Verne and Camille Flammarion happened to meet him and, taking him by the hand, led him gently forward. Before them caracoled the white horseman, his concentrated manner indicating that he was perfectly aware of his imminent appointment as future cedilla.

Having ascended at length the convolutions of a little white path they at last found themselves in full glory. At that moment the peace of infinity took hold of the great man. A glory lost more than thirty years before, that glory whose dense centre he was, and which emitted blinding rays to bathe the blind, completely surrounded him. This time he had become the target of the flashing arrows, it was towards him that they converged from all points of an unbounded space. Justice was done. With this rediscovered glory came tranquillity , the tranquillity he had vainly and expeditiously sought in life.

But to this peace, this tranquillity of a goal finally reached, was soon to be added even further bliss. Raymond Roussel realised that his thoughts were now travelling effortlessly along the difficult pathways that had once led him to write certain of his books. Those exhausting, laborious, dedicated researches which had erected between the external world and himself a thin curtain of steel, impenetrable to the most subtle of human rays, that voluntary and constant torture he knew to be the price of his exceptional genius, all were even now evaporating from his memory like the fading dream of a re-buffed suitor. Within him there began to seethe the outlines of so many masterpieces, to be added effortlessly to their predecessors, that he doubted the cogency of that inordinate glory. Was it perhaps only to be applied to his terrestial work? In future, the external world corresponding to his own world, he would have to do no more than describe what he saw, than follow with an intoxicated ease the course of his thoughts, which progressed quite naturally from thoughts (ideas) to marvels (surprising things) to thoughts (flowers) to marvels (a sort of fried paste sliced up into scenery).

Later on Roussel became very friendly with God, whom he successfully mimicked for his closest friends, a feat that earned him extra prestige among the angels.

—1953

MICHEL LEIRIS
Conception and Reality in the Work of Raymond Roussel

Translation   John Ashbery

On December 16, 1922 (a few days before the premiere of *Locus Solus* which took place in a tumult, before an almost entirely hostile public), Raymond Roussel sent me the following note:

"Thank you, my dear Michel, for your interesting and curious letter.

I see that, like me, you prefer the domain of Conception to that of Reality.

The interest which you are kind enough to show in my work is a proof to me that in you I meet again with the affection your father lavished on me, and I am deeply touched.

Yours affectionately."

In the fragment of Dr. Pierre Janet's work which Roussel reprints in *Comment j'ai écrit certains de mes livres* (pp. 175-183: "The Psychological Characteristics of Ecstasy") we find this remark concerning "Martial", that is to say Raymond Roussel, whom the famous psychiatrist treated for several years and described under this name (borrowed from the principal character in *Locus Solus*, the inventor Martial Canterel): "Martial has a very interesting conception of literary beauty. The work must contain nothing real, no observations on the world or the mind, nothing but completely imaginary combinations: these are already the ideas of an extra-human world." In another part of the same work (*De L'Angoisse à l'Extase*, vol. II, p. 515) Dr. Pierre Janet notes again: " 'If there was anything real in those descriptions,' said Martial, 'it would be ugly.' "

Finally, toward the end of the prefatory text to *Comment j'ai écrit...*, Roussel notes (after paying homage to the writer whom he considered his master, that is, Jules Verne): "I have travelled a great deal. Notably in 1920-21, I travelled around the world by way of India, Australia, New Zealand, the Pacific archipelagi, China, Japan and America . . . I already knew the principal countries of Europe, Egypt and all of North Africa, and later I visited Constantinople, Asia Minor and Persia. Now, from all these voyages I never took a single thing for my books. It seemed to me that the circumstance deserves mention, since it proves so well how imagination counts for everything in my work."

Thus, from a letter in which he alludes fleetingly to his aesthetic ideals, from confidences recorded in the medical notes of Dr. Pierre Janet, and, further, from this statement in a text intended to be published only post-humously, as befits a literary testament, it emerges that Roussel banked consistently on the imagination, and that for him there was a clear antithesis between the invented world which is that of "conception" and the given world —the human world in which we live our daily lives and which we cover in our travels—which is that of "reality".

As for reality, it is certain that Roussel—conscious nevertheless of having received a lion's share of it in the form of his immense fortune—expected nothing good to come of it.

Physical pain disturbed him, and my mother has told me how one day Roussel questioned her for a long time about the pains of giving birth, amazed that she had allowed it to be repeated since she had told him it was a very painful affair; in view of the period and Roussel's customary reserve, the subject must have meant a great deal to him for him to feel that he could discuss it thus with a woman still relatively young and little accustomed to talk about such questions. Mme Charlotte Dufrêne, who was his closest friend and to whom the posthumous work *Comment j'ai écrit...* is dedicated, told me in another connection that he had asked her never to speak to him of her fear of the dentist (nor of that she had of serpents) because he was afraid that she might, through contagion, infect him with her fears. Mme Dufrêne also declared to me that he was unable to bear the sight of tears.

Marcel Jean and Arpad Mezei (*Genèse de la Pensée Moderne*, p. 192) have noted that, in his works, Roussel seems to picture only objects sheltered from dust, and Pierre Schneider ("La Fenêtre ou Piège à Roussel," *Les Cahiers du Sud*, nos. 306-7) defines his art as "a poetry of high noon, in which objects cast no shadow around them," this in symbolic fashion since, in fact, night and shadow are far from absent in Roussel's work, just as scatology, or the bringing into play of disgusting elements among others, plays a role in it also. These remarks on certain general traits of his work seem to be confirmed in his life, as well, by that kind of dirt-phobia which Mme Charlotte Dufrêne—to whom I am indebted for much of my information—noticed in Raymond Roussel: before the first World War, it was his rule to wear his detachable collars only once (since he had a horror of laundered articles), his shirts a few times only; a suit, an overcoat, suspenders fifteen times; a necktie three times; and when he was clothed entirely in new clothes, he used to say: "I am on pins and needles—everything is new today."

Daily contact with a reality which to him seemed strewn with pitfalls obliged Roussel to take a number of precautions. During a certain period of his life when he suffered anguish whenever he happened to be in a tunnel, and was anxious to know at all times where he was, he avoided travelling at night; the idea that the act of eating is harmful to one's "serenity" also led him, during one period, to fast for days on end, after which he would break his fast by going to Rumpelmeyer's and devouring a vast quantity of cakes (corresponding to his taste for childish foods: marshmallows, milk, bread pudding, racahout); certain places to which he was attached by particularily happy childhood memories were taboo for him: Aix-les-Bains, Luchon, Saint-Moritz and the Hotel Beaurivage at Ouchy; also, afraid of being injured or causing injury in conversations, he used to say that in order to avoid all dangerous talk with people, he proceded by asking them questions.

In his investigation of the case of Martial, Dr. Pierre Janet mentions a phobia of disparagement and reproduces (*De l'Angoisse à L'Extase*, vol. II, p. 146 ff.) this declaration which shows how painful for Roussel must have been the almost total incomprehension which, for his part, he met with: "It's horrible that people don't respect acquired glory; a single detractor is stronger in my eyes than three million admirers; I must have unanimity for my mind to be at rest." Roussel, according to the same author, was a prey to a kind of "phobia of cheapening, linked to what he called 'the loss of the inaccessible' ": over and above any puritanical point of view, he disapproved, for instance, of bare breasts being displayed in the music halls (as a cheapening of what, in order to keep its charm, should remain a "forbidden fruit"), and he deplored mechanical progress which devalued travel by bringing it within everyone's range: "One only gambles when one is sure of breaking the bank; the happiness of others makes one suffer." Finally, Roussel's misoneism (*ibid.*, p. 230) had as a corollary his cult of precedents: "Everything that is new disturbs me," he would say, and so profound was his horror of change that, according to Charlotte Dufrêne, it would happen that having once performed a certain act, he would perform it again because the precedent thus formed had the force of an obligation.

From this strategy which he was forced to use in dealing with reality in order to adapt himself to it as best he could, resulted what Roussel himself called his "rule-omania" (*ibid.*, p. 200), that is, a need to arrange everything according to rules devoid of any ethical character, rules in their pure state, just as the rules to which he conformed in his writing seem exempt from any actual aesthetic intention. "His life was constructed like his books," Dr. Janet told me in the course of a conversation I had with him, several months after the death of the man from whom the celebrated psychiatrist had received many confidences, but whom he considered (in his own words) as a "poor, sick little fellow," completely failing to recognize his genius.

In the course of a trip he made through Persia in the year 1346 of the Hegira (according to the date on a postcard sent from Ispahan), Roussel sent Charlotte Dufrêne from Baghdad a postcard on which could be seen, moving along a wall apparently made of baked mud, three donkeys with packs led by a man in a white tunic and turban, with, on the left, a few trees including some palm-trees: "Here I am in Baghdad in the land of The Thousand and One Nights and Ali Baba, which reminds me of Lecocq; the people wear costumes more extraordinary than those of the chorus at the Gaîté." Roussel seems to have paid no attention whatever to the reality of Baghdad; all that counted for him was the city of his imagination: scarcely even that of the folk tales of The Thousand and One Nights—rather that which had appeared to him when he saw at the Gaîté-Lyrique theatre Lecocq's operetta based on the tale of Ali Baba.

Literarily, it seems that Roussel proceeds always as though it were necessary for there to be the maximum number of screens between nature and himself, so that one might in this case compare him to great aesthetes like Baudelaire and Wilde, for whom art was categorically opposed to nature; but, with Roussel, everything happens as though one should retain of art only the inventiveness, that is the share of pure conception by which art distinguishes itself from nature. In all his work, one notes that the plot (the structure of the work or its point of departure) is of an artificial, not a natural character. as Pierre Schneider has pointed out (*op. cit.*), the poem "Mon Ame" which subsequently became "L'Ame de Victor Hugo," written by Roussel at the age of 17 and published in the *Gaulois* of July 12, 1897, a poem which is constructed on the line: "My soul is a strange factory," is nothing more than the development of a banal metaphor of the type: "My soul is an Infanta in her court-dress..." and it has as its subject poetic creation itself likened to the stratagems of a creating god; the novel in verse *La Doublure*—during the writing of which Roussel experienced that sensation of "universal glory" which he described to Pierre Janet—has for its theme the story of an actor and consists primarily of a description of the maskers and floats of the Carnival at Nice; the three poems "La Vue," "La Scource" and "Le Concert" describe, not actual spectacles, but three pictures: a photograph set in a pen holder, the label on a bottle of mineral water, a vignette in the letterhead of a sheet of writing paper; far from referring to the Africa of travellers, *Impressions d'Afrique* hinges on a fête of a theatrical character given on the occasion of a coronation; *Locus Solus* is the account of a walk through a park full of wonderful inventions; in the play *L'Etoile au Front*, a series of curios forms the pretext for a string of anecdotes and, in *La Poussière de Soleils* it is a question of a chain of enigmas which lead to the discovery of a treasure; *Nouvelles Impressions d'Afrique* is nothing more than meditations on four tourist attractions of modern Egypt; finally, of the texts collected in *Comment j'ai écrit...*, some are given as illustrations of the eminently artificial method of creation explained in the prologue, the others refer to the Carnival at Nice, with the exception of the six *Documents pour servir de Canevas*, which are of the story-within-a-story type so abundantly represented in Roussel's work and which—like the composition with more or less indefinitely prolonged parentheses peculiar to *Nouvelles Impressions d'Afrique*—seems to have served in the most literal way his need to multiply the screens.

In the preamble to *Comment j'ai écrit...*, Roussel sets forth the completely arbitrary process which he used for writing his prose works, including the plays; he tried nothing similar for the writings in verse, perhaps because the separation, the distance, the departure from reality was provided by the very fact of expressing himself in verse, without its thus being necessary to resort to additional artifice. "This process is in short related to rhyme. In both cases, there is unforseen creation due to phonic combinations." And reading these lines of Roussel, one thinks of what Racan wrote in his *Life of Malherbe*: "The reason he gave for the necessity of rhyming widely differing words rather than the customary ones was that one happened on more beautiful verses by bringing the former together, rather than by rhyming those whose meaning was almost similar; and he made a point of seeking out rare and sterile rhymes, believing as he did that they engendered new ideas, not to mention the fact that it was a mark of the great poet to attempt difficult rhymes which had never been rhymed before." In reality, it seems that Roussel's assertion is merely a theoretical justification, and that (except perhaps in regard to "Mon Ame", the first and most "inspired" of his poems, and which he regarded as his fundamental work), rhyme never played for him the role of a catalyst the way puns did, for, in examining the texture of his verse works, one does not see how rhyme could have served him as a propelling force; one would say, on the contrary, that he put into verse works which might have well been written in prose.

However that may be, the following is the process, in its various forms, which provided Roussel with the elements he used in his prose tales:

1. First, two phrases, identical except for one word, with a play on the double meanings of other substantives in both phrases. "Once the two phrases had been found," Roussel indicates, "it was a question of writing a story

which could begin with the first and end with the second."

Example: *Les vers* (The lines of verse) *de la doublure* (of the understudy) *dans la pièce* (in the play) *du Forban Talon Rouge* (of "Red-Heel the Buccaneer") and *Les vers* (The worms) *de la doublure* (in the lining) *de la pièce* (of the patch) *du fort pantalon rouge* (of the heavy red trousers)—which forms the basis of the story "Chiquenaude", published in 1900, the first work which the author considered satisfactory after the profound nervous depression which followed the failure of the novel *La Doublure.*

2. A word with two meanings joined to another word with two meanings by the preposition *à*—with—(which becomes the instrument of association of two absolutely dissimilar elements, just as the conjunction *as* is used to associ-ate two more or less similar elements in the classical metaphor by analogy.)

Example: *Palmier* (a kind of cake, or a palm-tree) *à restauration* (a restaurant where cakes are served or the restoration of a dynasty on a throne), a pair of words which, in *Impressions d'Afrique,* produces the palm-tree of the Square of Trophies consecrated to the restoration of the Talou dynasty.

3. A random phrase "from which I drew images by distorting it, a little as though it were a case of deriving them from the drawings of a rebus."

Example: *Hellstern, 5 Place Vendôme,* the address of Roussel's shoe-maker, deformed into *hélice tourne zinc plat se rend dôme*—"propeller turns zinc flat goes dome"—which furnished the elements of an apparatus manipulated by the emperor Talou's eldest son *(ibid.)*

In the works of Raymond Roussel elaborated according to this method, literary creation thus includes a first stage which consists in establishing a sentence or expression with a double meaning, or else in "dislocating" a phrase which already exists; the elements to be confronted with each other and brought into play are thus engendered by these fortuitous formal aspects. After the intermediate stage which is constituted by a logical plot joining these elements together, no matter how disparate they may be, comes the formulation of these relationships on as realistic a level as possible, in a text written with the utmost rigour, with no other attempt at style than the strictest application of the conventional rules, with concision and the absence of repetitions of terms coming at the head of the list of objectives pursued. This concern for extreme rigour in the production of works of which the least one can say is that they are far removed indeed from any kind of naturalism is reminiscent of an epigram of Juan Gris, the most rationalistic and at the same time one of the greatest of the Cubist painters: "One must be inexact but precise." The deferential obedience to the rules of good language such as they are taught in a lycee confirms in another connection the correctness of a remark of Marcel Duchamp, who, speaking to me of Roussel and his special erudition, said that he was a "secondary" the way that others are "elementary."

It should be noted that this abstention from any strictly stylistic effects led Roussel to an extraordinary transparency of style.

In *Nouvelles Impressions d'Afrique,* the detachment from the real which Roussel seems to have aimed at is obtained in quite another way: the dislocation of the phrase by means of parentheses introducing a practically infinite series of "false bottoms," breaking up, parceling out, disarticulating the thread of the meaning until one loses it. In his analysis of the second canto of *Nouvelles Impressions*, a work destined to become a classic among Rousselian studies, Jean Ferry very justly writes that "even more than the famous Japanese box whose cubes fit exactly one into the other down to the tiniest of them all, the composition evokes two or three large concentric spheres, between whose surfaces, unequally distant, might float other spheres themselves having several layers," an image taken up in a recent article by Renato Mucci for whom there is no Rousselian work in which the end and the beginning do not join each other as is the case in these poems whose single sentence is cut up by multiple parentheses to which footnotes have been grafted, each of these works appearing as a differentiated unity which, throughout the series of elements peculiar to it, takes on a value of concrete universality in turning back upon itself.

Not only does the process employed by Roussel for the composition of his prose works have the immense interest of adding up to a deliberate promotion of language to the rank of creative agent, instead of contenting itself with using it as an agent of execution, but it seems that the subjugation to a specious and arbitrary law (obliging a concentration on the difficult resolution of a problem whose given facts are. as *independent* as possible of each other) has as a consequence a distraction whose liberating power appears much more efficacious than the abandon, pure and simple, implied by the use of a process like automatic writing. Aiming at an almost total detachment from everything that is nature, feeling and humanity, and working laboriously over materials apparently so gratuitous that they were not suspect to him, Roussel arrived by this paradoxical method at the creation of *authentic* myths, in which his affectivity is reflected in a more or less direct or symbolic way, as is shown by the frequency of certain themes which constitute the leitmotivs of his work and of which the omnipotence of science, the close relation between microcosm and macrocosm, ecstasy, Eden, the treasure to be discovered or the riddle to be solved, artificial survival and post mortem states, masks and costumes, as well as many themes which could be interpreted as stemming from fetichism or sado-masochism, constitute examples (here enumerated without any attempt at a methodical inventory). It is not an exaggeration to say that the establishing of a thematic index of Roussel's work might allow one to discover a psychological content equivalent to those of most of the great western mythologies; this, because the products of Roussel's imagination are, in a way, *quintessential commonplaces*: disconcerting and singular as it may be for the public, he drew on the same sources as popular imagination and childish imagination and, in addition, his culture was essentially popular and childish (melodramas, serial stories, operettas, vaudeville, fairy tales, stories in pictures, etc.) as are his processes (stories within stories, set forms of words used as the structure for a tale, and down to his method of creation by dramatized puns—the literary equivalent of the mechanism used in certain social diversions, charades, for example). No doubt the almost unanimous incomprehension which Roussel unfortunately encountered resulted less from an inability to attain universality than from this bizarre combination of the "simple as ABC" with the quintessential.

Using childish and popular forms to express his own profundity, Roussel reaches down into a common storehouse, and it is thus not surprising that the personal myths he elaborated are liable to converge (as Michel Carrouges maintains) on certain great occult sequences in western thought; so that it is, to say the least, superfluous to explain (as does André Breton in his preface to Jean Ferry) why the scenario of *La Poussière de Soleils* can seem to be based on the traditional evolution of the alchemists' search for the Philosopher's Stone by suggesting that Roussel might have been an adept of hermetic philosophy. In view of the rules of secrecy which the initiates observe (a rule to which Roussel as an initiate would have been by definition subjected, confining himself, in accordance with the custom, to revealing it in an occult way), such a hypothesis escapes refutation and one can only argue, in order to reject it, the absence of any profession of faith of this kind, in his conversation as well as in his writings; still, the fact remains that in spite of certain aspects of Roussel's work (the important role played by techniques of divination, the frequent use of legendary and marvelous elements), this work utterly lacking in effects of shading has an essentially positivist colouring and that nothing we know of this writer of genius—not even the phrase in which he was illumined by a sensation of "universal glory"—inclines one to attribute him aspirations of a mystical nature.

When Roussel had a kind of skylight built into his mother's coffin so as to be able to observe her face to the last moment, and when he imagined the refrigerator in *Locus Solus* in which corpses, thanks to scientific processes, relive the crowning incident of their lives, he was recording, no doubt, his refusal to accept death, but recording it as an unbeliever for whom nothing exists after our corporeal existence is finished. Evidence of a deep attachment to his own physical person is provided both by his taste for elegant clothing (an elegance which, in its sobriety, was literally all-important for him) and by the troublesome treatment which he underwent, even during his trip in Persia, when he began to be obsessed by the fear that his hair was getting white. If, when conversing with the late Eugène Vallée (the chief typesetter of the Lemerre printing house who worked on the composition of all his books and who, like almost all those who had any contact with Roussel, spoke of him as the simplest and most charming of beings), he frequently indulged in estimates of the probable time that each of them still had to live, it was to statistical data that he referred for these calculations and, deep as his obsession was, it was a scientific point of view that he adopted. Such a scientific approach allied to a passionate desire to expand, not on a mystical but on the material level, the limits which are imposed on man, is found again in his admiration for Camille Flammarion (to the point where he had a tiny transparent box in the form of a star specially constructed, to conserve a little cake of the same shape brought home from a lunch at which, on July 29, 1923, he was a guest of the illustrious astronomer at the Observatory of Juvisy), in his identification with the inventor Martial Canterel, in his interest in Einstein's theory of relativity, and in his certitude—which he confided to his friend Charlotte Dufrène—that a day would come when men would discover a means of travel by re-ascending the course of time. As for the pleasure he took in visiting crèches at Christmas time and altars on Good Friday, and in attending High Mass at Easter, this is probably nothing more than the expression of his fondness for folklore and, perhaps, that of his attachment to a childhood of which he wrote that he had a "delightful memory." Similarily the edifying and marvelous tales which abound in his work are always presented between ethnographic or historiographic quotation marks. Finally, that very sensation of "universal glory" which he declares having experienced while writing *La Doublure* (and which he was anxious to know whether certain well-known writers had experienced also) is not a spiritual state but something felt physically, an intoxication, a "euphoria," (which he sought in drugs after having sought it momentarily in alcohol, after becoming certain of not finding it while writing), a satisfaction which seems quite close to that "serenity" in whose name he paid his chess instructor's debts: thus, if it is in card games he found serenity . . .

It seems in short that if Roussel declared that he preferred "the domain of Conception to that of Reality," the world which he thus contrasted to that of everyday life had no belief in the supernatural at its base. In *Comment j'ai écrit...*, Roussel prides himself on being a logician and one must admit that his essential ambition of a man pursuing "euphoria" in the almost demigod-like exercise of his intellect, was to be the champion of the imagination: a Victor Hugo, a Jules Verne, a phenomenal chess player, an Oedipus solving riddles (leading one to wonder whether the riddles which perhaps still remain to be deciphered in his work are not perhaps of the same order as those which he solved with great pride at the Théâtre du Petit Monde, where he used to go with his friend Charlotte Dufrene, taking along a little girl of their acquaintance to serve as an alibi.) His effort tends towards the creation of a fictive world, entirely fabricated, having nothing in common with reality; where he succeeds in creating truth by the force of his genius alone, without having recourse to some further reality. Logically, this supremely negative effort—to cut the bonds which might be able to attach his conceptual world to reality—was to lead Raymond Roussel, who was no idealist, to the definitive disengagement which is voluntary death. This seems to be what he had always dimly felt, as is borne out by this addition "from earliest youth" to a poem by Victor Hugo (*Comment j'ai écrit..*, p.38):

Comment, disaient-ils	How, they asked
Nous sentant des ailes	Feeling that we have wings
Quitter ces corps vils?	Shall we leave these vile bodies?
—Mourez, disaient-elles.	Die, they replied.

In 1932 Raymond Roussel had stopped writing. He had taken up chess and was drugging himself with soporifics (barbiturates).

On April 16 he gave the printer the main part of his "secret and posthumous" work dedicated to Charlotte Dufrène.

At that time he had ceased to live in his sister's private mansion in the Rue Quentin-Bauchart, and had taken up residence at 75 Rue Pigalle in a residential hotel frequented by homosexuals and drug addicts, that is by people who shared the exclusive taste he had always had, and his more recent passion for drugs.

On December 24 he attended Midnight Mass at Notre-Dame-de-Lorette with his companions.

Returning from the African tropics toward the beginning of 1933, I went to call on Roussel who had been one of the patrons of the scientific mission of which I was a member. He received me, as he had since he had given up his house at Neuilly, at the home of Charlotte Dufrène in the rue Pierre-Charron. Clad in an extremely dark grey, if not completely black, suit, he was wearing the decoration of the Legion of Honour (this, at least, of his ambitions had been fulfilled, although he had been unable to have his photograph in an album of celebrities published by Mariani wine, or have a street named after him). He had shaved his moustache; still handsome and elegant, but somewhat heavier and slumping a bit, he seemed to be speaking from very far away. He had not seen me for some two years and asked me successively for news of a large number of my relatives. A melancholy reflection (with a smile) on life: "It goes by faster and faster!" After I said goodbye to him, he accompanied me into the anteroom and we stood talking for a long time (according to his habit—was it shyness? fear of seeming to show me out?— of keeping people with him long after saying goodbye). During the same visit, when I asked him whether he had been writing, he replied: "It's so difficult!"

On May 30, 1933, before leaving for Sicily, he made detailed arrangements for a posthumous volume, in a series of four notes written at the Lemerre printing house.

In Palermo he took up residence at the Grande Albergo e delle Palme, room 226, communicating with number 227 (occupied by Charlotte Dufrène, his "housekeeper") at the corner of the Via Mariano Stabile and the Via Riccardo Wagner, the quietest part of the building, in which Richard Wagner had lived on the first floor while writing *Parsifal*, and where Francesco Crispi, the statesman, had also lived, as is mentioned in two plaques.

Roussel used to say that, except during childhood, he had never had an hour of happiness and described his anguish as a kind of suffocation, a gasping for breath. But in Palermo he found complete "euphoria"; he was no longer preoccupied with his "glory" which had not been recognized, nor with his writing; he said that he would give the whole world for a moment of euphoria. "Cut, cut, but give me my drug!" he said one day when he was deprived of drugs, meaning that the amputation of his two arms and legs would have been preferable to such a deprivation.

According to Charlotte Dufrène, Roussel when drugged had a taste for death, which before had frightened him.

One morning around seven o'clock, he was found bleeding in his bath; he had opened his veins with a razor, and he burst out laughing, saying, "How easy it is to open one's veins... It's nothing at all." Later, when the drug had worn off, he wondered how he could have done this.

Several days after arriving in Palermo he had begged Charlotte Dufrêne to return to Paris to dismiss his servants (whom he had amply remunerated) and asked her also to liquidate his apartment, so as to be rid of everything he still possessed in Paris, his intention being to travel and not to return for a long time.

He was at this time so weak that he could scarcely eat. He slept on a mattress placed on the floor, afraid of falling out of bed while under the influence of drugs. The reason he gave for not wanting to eat was that it disturbed his "serenity."

One day he had Charlotte Dufrêne write to his man-servant, asking him to send a case with a certain number, and he said that this case contained a revolver which he wanted sent to him because as a foreigner he could not (or so he thought) buy one in Palermo. He told his friend that unfortunately he would not have the courage to press the trigger, and that perhaps she would do it for him. As she tried to thrust aside this idea, he attempted to make her give in by bringing out his chequebook and asked her how much she wished; after each refusal he raised the sum. In the end the letter was not sent.

At Mme Dufrêne's insistence, Roussel finally decided to go to Kreuzlingen in Switzerland to be cured. On the morning of July 13 he had a telegraph sent to this effect. In the evening he told his companion that she could go to sleep in peace, as he was feeling well that day and had taken no soporifics. For several days the connecting door had been shut at night, whereas before it had remained open.

On the morning of the 14th, not hearing any noise, Mme Dufrêne knocked on the door between the two rooms. Obtaining no answer, she called a servant. The latter entered by the door from the corridor, which was unlocked. Mme Dufrêne and the servant found Roussel stretched out on his mattress which he had pushed or dragged as far as the connecting door (representing a superhuman effort in view of his weakened condition). His face was calm, restful and turned toward that door.

In order to bring the body back from Palermo it was necessary to embalm it.

In the theatrical adaption of the novel *Locus Solus*, one of the chief attractions of the spectacle was the "Ballet of Glory": the suicide of a misunderstood poet, whom one subsequently sees enter into immortality—an immortality which is, of course, by no means that of the other world but the purely civic immortality of the world of statues, monuments and street-names. One cannot refrain from emphasizing that it was at the foot of a communicating door—that which led to the room of his friend and confidante —that Roussel had insisted on dying (unless it was that before his privation he had wanted to experience to the utmost the euphoria that the soporifics gave him). Whatever may have been his immediate motive and the reason for which he had chosen such a position—was it to be close to the door or to barricade it?—he died by his own hand on the very threshold of that *communication* which he had recognized as impossible, at least during his life, and with his eyes turned towards the place occupied by the only person, apparently, who had shared a little, but only a little, in his intimacy.

—1954

Roussel's nephew and heir, Michel Ney, with Roussel's dog, Pipo, who is smoking a pipe.

JOHN ASHBERY
Introduction to Raymond Roussel's "In Havana"

Translation   John Ashbery

The text which follows is apparently the first unpublished work of Raymond Roussel to be discovered up to now.[1] It was intended to be the first chapter of Roussel's last, unfinished novel, which was published minus this opening chapter in his posthumous collection, *How I Wrote Some of My Books* under the title *Documents to Serve as a Framework.* In addition to its purely literary attractiveness, the fragment presents a number of peculiarities.

The first is that it survived at all. The published *Documents* were preceded by a note from Roussel dated 15 January 1932:

"If I die before having completed this work and in case someone wishes to publish it even in its unfinished state, I desire that the beginning be suppressed, and that it begin with the First Document, which follows, and that the initials be replaced by names which will fill in the blanks, and that it be given a general title: *Documents to Serve as a Framework.*

Nonetheless the publisher Lemerre had begun by printing the beginning Roussel later wanted to suppress: the proofs for most of it are extant, and for the last few lines, a handwritten note which has turned up among papers of Roussel discovered since his death. The fact that at the time he wrote the note in January 1932 he had finished only six of the thirty Documents which were to make up the novel leads one to believe that at his death in July 1933 he had still not made a definitive decision to keep or suppress the first chapter: perhaps he had it printed so early on in order to give himself time to reflect on the matter.

For several reasons I have decided not to observe Roussel's stated desire that the chapter not be published. First and most important, it seems to me that any text by Roussel deserves to be known. In addition it appears obvious that it was not doubts about the quality of the work that prompted Roussel to write the note quoted above, but a simple desire for symmetry: shorn of their introduction, the six 'documents' form an easily publishable whole.

The personality of the writer furnishes an additional justification: it is well known that he was haunted by the idea of posthumous glory. "This glory will shine on all my works without exception; it will reflect on all the events of my life; people will look up the details of my childhood and admire the way I played prisoner's base," he confided to Dr. Pierre Janet, who treated him. Since the glory that was to come was the great consolation of his unhappy life, we might conclude that the publication of this text would not have displeased him.

The first chapter sheds new light on the *Documents* it was meant to precede and which are, in my opinion, one of Roussel's most remarkable works? We now see that the novel was to take place in Cuba, but that it was interrupted almost at the beginning by a series of digressions (as in *Impressions of Africa* and *Locus Solus*). Each of the chapters is made up in turn of dozens of very short narratives, adroitly dovetailed, which form the actual fabric of the novel. Each document, we now see, is an illustration of the superiority of Europe over America and is the result of patient research by a member of the club of which M... is the female president.

However, the mysterious aspects of the work, those surrounding the coded meanings in which it seems so rich, those resulting from Roussel's method of composition and the very nature of his writing (of which he left only a brief explanation in his essay, "How I Wrote Some of My Books") cannot be explained merely by his known techniques of construction. On the single galley proof which comprises the text, proper names are left blank and replaced by initials, while dates are omitted.[3] No doubt this will provide those who believe Roussel's work to be one vast and theoretically decipherable riddle with a persuasive argument. The presence of the initials and the absence of any name or date strongly suggest the use of a code. This hypothesis is all the more plausible given Roussel's well-known passion for mystery and mystifications, cryptograms, ciphers and other tools of secrecy.

Thus, to start with commonplace phrases, deform them, obtain phrases that are very close phonetically and use the latter as elements of a narrative, is to use a code. Moreover, references to ciphers and clues abound in his work: the *'grille'* or cipher-stencil that figures in the story of the Zouave in *Impressions of Africa* reappears in the Fifth Document, where the soldier Armand Vage inherits from a wealthy sister "a piece of cardboard pierced with two holes, which could only be a stencil meant to lead to the discovery of a treasure." (More of him later.)

As regards style, the text has the same radical concision and the peculiar transparency of the *Documents*. After the acrobatics of *New Impressions of Africa,* with its interlaced parenthetical passages inserted willy-nilly in the procrustean bed of the alexandrine, Roussel's prose reaffirms its rigor, even more marked here than in *Locus Solus*. He submits his sentences to processes of condensation that result in amazing verbal crystallizations. Furthermore he imposes a new discipline on himself by forcing each of the episodes of his book to fulfill a narrative function: A...'s "measure of authority" serves the same story-spinning purpose in this prefatory chapter as does the superiority of Europe in the Documents themselves. Incidentally the procedure recalls the 'lists of examples' in *New Impressions of Africa.*

In the course of these few pages we come upon a number of motifs and words dear to Roussel. Among the former are the passionate friendship of two siblings (recalling Séil-Kor and Nina in *Impressions of Africa*, Fermoir and Tige in "The Coils of the Great Serpent," and perhaps Roussel's deep affection for his own sister when they were children); the theme of twins (the "Espagnolettes" of *Impressions of Africa*) of unequal growth (the rubber tree and the palm in the same book); the *catin* (harlot, strumpet) who appears in *New Impressions* and throughout Roussel's work) with a past described as *houleux* (turbulent, chequered): Jean Ferry correctly cites the latter as one of Roussel's favourite adjectives. Moreover the setting of the book, *Havana, Cuba* hints at a coarse play on words. Concerning the scatological element in *New Impressions*, Ferry wrote in his book-length essay on the poem: "I shall limit myself to pointing out Roussel's extraordinary prudery with regard to this sort of subject matter in his earlier works. I should very much like to know, once others have studied and resolved the problem, what sluices burst in him on this occasion, causing these malodorous streams to run together." But it seems to me that these references had already appeared, in hidden form, in previous works. Among the objects ornamenting the Square of Trophies in *Impressions of Africa* is a small privy-like building whose gently sloping roof is made of *feuillets* ('leaves' but also 'sheets of toilet paper') taken from the book *The Fair Maid of Perth* (the French pronunciation of Perth is the same as that of *pertes*, a type of vaginal discharge); several portraits of the Electors of Brandenbourg ('Brandebourg', the gallicized version of the place-name, might be a pun on *bran de bourg*:'town excrement'): and a watercolour depicting the "immoral" Flore training her lorgnette (the phrase is *"braquer sa lorgnette"*, transformable into a spoonerism, *lorgner sa braguette*: 'ogle his codpiece') on an actor performing on a stage. One could cite other examples that seem to suggest that the solemn facade of Roussel's prose style is in fact riddled with puns, spoonerisms and other *jeux de mots* which are often of an obscene nature.[4]

But 'Cuba'; the 'Club' with its thirty members, each charged with the mission of "providing the handsomest stone for the edifice"; as well as the fact that, of a total of thirty documents, only six were completed, bring us once again to that 'cube' that occurs throughout Roussel's work, and whose possible meaning is suggested by André Breton in his preface to Ferry's *Essay on Raymond Roussel*. "The cube . . . represents one of Roussel's chief preoccupations and one of the main clues in his play [*The Dust of Suns*], and is also one of the capital stages in the production of the philosopher's stone . . . Fulcanelli, in his work on alchemy, reproduces the image of a cubical stone secured by ropes that is part of a bas-relief decoration of the St. Martin fountain, a few steps from the theatre where *The Dust of Suns* was performed." And a similar stone makes a striking appearance in the Fifth Document: "On his twenty-first try, struck by the words 'cube' and 'mesmerize' [*méduser*], perfectly framed by the two holes in the stencil, Armand Vage abstained from further meditative reading: '*A cube would mesmerize him.*' Having lifted a remarkably cubical mossy stone at the edge of a brook that ran through his sister's garden, he discovered a substantial hoard."[5]

One hesitates before a number of possible interpretations. The puns suggested by this "Cuba" where the novel is situated make one wonder whether Roussel hasn't proceeded 'alchemically' on several levels: that of the psychological unconscious (sublimation of *shameful* material by the work of art); that of language—Cuba for *cul bas* (posterior), *Havane* (the French word for a shade of tan) for the colour of excrement; and finally that of alchemy itself in Breton's sense.

The text presents a further singularity. At the end of the chapter, M..., looking for a costume befitting her role as president of a club founded to publicize the glory of Europe, has a sudden inspiration. "Among some Dresden porcelains displayed from time immemorial in a vitrine in her parlour was one that depicted the Rape of Europa.[6] A graceful garment, closely modelled after that of the statuette—and completed by a flesh-coloured leotard—became her presidential uniform." Curiously, a Dresden figurine representing the Rape of Europa figured in the important art collection of Mme. Roussel, the writer's mother. A photograph of it is reproduced in the lavish catalogue printed for the sale of the collection, which was organized by Roussel and his sister in 1912, shortly after their mother's death. This porcelain was then an object that Roussel himself had seen "from time immemorial" in his mother's salon (it is perhaps worth pointing out that her name, Marguerite, begins with an M), and is not a figment of his imagination. Yet we know that Roussel made it a rule to exclude all reality from his work; Janet writes: "Martial [Roussel] has a very interesting conception of beauty in literature: the work of art must contain nothing real, no observation of the real or spiritual world, only totally imaginary arrangements." For a reason we cannot know, Roussel here uses an existing object, a porcelain statuette sold at auction twenty years earlier. One could hardly deduce the presence of an autobiographical element in his work from the circumstance, but it is nonetheless interesting since it suggests that the relationship between the life and work of this most secretive of French writers may be less disjoined than was previously supposed. The details we possess concerning that life are, alas, minimal, but it is always possible that new facts will be revealed which will shed further light on an oeuvre so carefully concealed behind enigmas of all kinds.

Will the cipher ever be decoded? Will the secret—philosopher's stone or 'hoard'—which those familiar with the work (Leiris, Breton, Ferry) agree that it conceals, ever be discovered? It is unlikely, despite the new clues that "In Havana" seems to contain. Doubtless the beauty of a work like this is directly linked to the obscurity of its author's intentions; its charm is rather like that of some antique mechanism constructed for a use that escapes us today. Perhaps the message Roussel wanted to leave with us boils down to this: the impossibility of knowing all; the possibility of a superior knowledge to which we will never attain.

—1962

Notes

The preceding article was published in the French review *L'Arc* in 1962. I wrote it in English and it was translated into French by a friend, the late Michel Thurlotte. My original text seems to have disappeared, so that for the purposes of this publication I have had to translate it from French back into English. [Author's note]

1. 1962. [Author's note]
2. Not everyone agrees: Rayner Heppenstall, in his *Raymond Roussel: A Critical Study*, sees in them signs of "deterioration of mind". [Author's note]
3. This was not a new practice for him: the names of characters were also left blank in the published version of "The Place of Red Buttons", one of the *Texts of Early Youth*. In the manuscript of the *Documents*, which I saw once at the home of some distant cousins of Roussel, dates were left blank and names indicated by an initial and a blank. But since the proofs have apparently not survived, it is impossible to know whether the names and dates were eventually supplied by Roussel or (as he had requested in his note) by another hand. The names *sound* Rousselian.

   Speaking of proofs, when I was beginning research on Roussel in about 1959 I went to the offices of Lemerre, which was then moribund but still extant, asking to see any papers they might have relating to Roussel. I was told that there were indeed files but that I would need the permission of a member of the family in order to examine them. I received this permission from Michel Ney, Roussel's nephew and heir, who accompanied me to the Lemerre offices, whereupon the same official I had spoken with previously told us that they had no Roussel papers! A few months later Lemerre shut down for good and its archives were, I believe, destroyed. [Author's note]

4. I am indebted to Pierre Martory for suggesting these possible plays on words, and also for discovering a copy of the catalogue of Mme. Roussel's art collection [see note 6] at a Paris flea-market, at a time when no one knew of its existence. [Author's note]

5. Strangely, Palermo, the city that Roussel seems to have chosen as his place of death, numbers among its curiosities a cubical castle of the Norman period known as "La Cuba". [Author's note]

6. The French phrase "L'Enlèvement d'Europe" could mean both "The Rape of Europa" and "Europe's Carrying off the Prize".

Mme. Roussel owned more than eighty Dresden figurines (as well as paintings by Gainsborough, Lawrence, Fragonard, Nattier, Greuze, Corot and others), including, in addition to "Europa", two allegorical figures representing America and Africa (see below). In my copy of the sale catalogue, someone jotted down both the estimates and the actual prices attained by the various lots at the auction: there, at least, America seems to have triumphed with a price of 12,500 francs, as against 1500 fetched by "The Rape of Europa". [Author's note]

"Africa" and "America":

"The Rape of Europa".

RAYMOND ROUSSEL
In Havana

Translation   John Ashbery

In Havana in the year   lived a pair of orphans, the fourteen-year-old A...
L... and his twin sister M....

Born to a Spanish colonial family, the two children grew up under the
affectionate tutelage of their maiden great-aunt S..., a capable, unpretentious
person, well-versed in managing her own affairs.

As is usual, the twins had grown unevenly in the maternal womb:
M... had absorbed many a vital essence, to the detriment of A..., who,
incurably fragile, had only by a miracle reached adolescence.

Between A... and M... reigned the fanatic tenderness typical of twins.
Moreover A..., extremely gifted, was able to exert a beneficial ascendancy
on his entourage, to which his sister wholeheartedly submitted. In school he
dominated the class, and, drawing additional prestige from the title
veteran, the result of a serious illness which had forced him to stay in a form
a second year, counselled some, sustained others, or settled the quarrels of
yet others with but a word or two.

Two examples will show the scope of his authority.

Among his friends he counted the son of N... O..., a parvenu well-known
throughout the land—and that of R... V..., whose name called to mind a
mysterious scandal.

A humble servant to a planter, N... O... had, with the aid of a lucky lottery
ticket, been able while still very young to lay the foundations of a fortune which,
thanks to his talents and avarice, had during a quarter of a century become
considerable.

But his origins had gained him nothing but the contempt of Cuban high
society, contempt from which he suffered and which he attempted to over-
come through the purchase of a title.

He left for Rome—and returned a papal count.

But the fashionable Cubans, not in the least impressed, saw this as a
provocation and took umbrage. Not only were the advances of the new noble-
man rebuffed, but it was agreed that he would be sent a syntax whose
luxurious binding was decorated with the ornate crest of a count. It was a
way of neatly twitting the pretensions of the unlettered former flunkey.

Count d'O... understood—and kept his peace.

Besides, other cares would soon preoccupy him.

Havana at the time was fêting an Italian opera company whose star was the beautiful and amoral A..., known as the "queen of the vocalise".

As the vocal repertory offered nothing sufficiently demanding to show off fully her remarkable virtuosity, A... had had arranged for voice, using lyrics suggested by the title, the "Spinning Song" for piano by D..., whose perilous chromatic runs, aiming at subtle imitative effects and forbidden to lesser talents, followed one another relentlessly. And the execution of the work, already a tour de force for the fingers, became for the vocal cords a miraculous exploit.

A... accomplished this feat effortlessly, attaining, while always singing pianissimo, an extreme velocity in which the phrasing of the separate notes that stretched out each syllable was never compromised.

At the end of each last act, urgent curtain-calls forced A... to sing her "Spinning Song", resulting invariably in a triumph.

The first time d'O... saw A... appear on stage, her dazzling beauty produced a delightful agitation in him which immediately increased twofold at the sound of her voice. His desire, swelling with each act of the opera, burst all bounds at the end when the customary "Spinning Song", adding the crowning touch to her prestige, caused her to surpass herself as a lyric artist and then radiate in a final apotheosis.

When after an easy conquest the totally ecstatic d'O... heard talk of the troupe's departure, his anguish revealed the depth of his passion. He made A... alluring offers in an attempt to persuade her to abandon the stage and remain with him, whereupon she ascertained her power and, deciding to exploit the situation to the hilt, refused him all save marriage and held out until he yielded.

The irruption into his existence of a wife with a chequered past only aggravated the ostracism from which d'O... suffered—and against which he decided to struggle yet another time.

It was on horse racing, much in vogue in Cuba, that he built his hopes. A racing stable would bring with it a certificate of smartness—and acquaintances in the brilliant society of the racing world.

He acquired a stable and, in A...'s honour, chose as his colours the green, white and red of the Italian flag, alert for every chance to support her with visible tributes against the disfavour of prudes.

But, if the couple had a few sporting successes in the hippodrome, these met with nothing but further snubs, and d'O..., chagrined, soon parted with all his horses.

This disappointment was followed by a joy: the birth of a son.

Now it was this son, S... d'O..., thirteen years old at the time of the story, who was a friend of A... L...'s.

A classmate having called S..., during a whispered argument at school, "son of a lackey and a strumpet", the youth had retorted with a challenge.

At the first sign of fisticuffs during recess, A... had intervened—then made inquiries.

Given the odious nature of the insult, he insisted that S... receive public apologies—and, as usual, was deferentially obeyed.

As for V...'s son, he had unjustly suffered the consequences of certain suspicions that hung over his father.

Orphaned at an early age, the latter had, on reaching his majority, rapidly dissipated a modest inheritance and, of comely aspect, then sought . . . and found an heiress.

A few years of high living melted the dowry away, and the irritated parents-in-law subsidized only meagerly the couple—henceforth beset by difficulties which the birth of a son only augmented. Now, scarcely had V...'s wife risen from childbed when her father and mother died mysteriously within the same hour.

The autopsy furnished proof of a double poisoning.

An investigation of foodstuffs having led to nought, it became necessary to look elsewhere. Suspicion finally settled on the glue of a supply of stamps of touching origin.

Two years previously the American T... had attempted, on his vessel the B..., an audacious polar exploration.

When the anticipated time of his return had been largely exceeded, a public subscription drive to finance a search party was launched.

Notably a stamp was created which, showing the B... lost amid floes, accompanied the franking stamp on many an envelope.

More than one hand was forced by the ploy of sending out an unsolicited sheet of a hundred stamps—for which a canvasser soon appeared, to request either the return of the sheet or a contribution.

Now a sheet of this type had reached the home of V...'s parents-in-law and been utilized at once, the canvasser having been welcomed on arrival.

It was two weeks afterward that they died.

Six stamps remained—and analysis proved the presence of poisoned glue.

Since no envelopes could be found, the investigation came up short—and foundered. But suspicions concerning the too-fortunate V... were bruited about—without touching his wife, who enjoyed universal esteem.

Since then, however, gossip had never ceased.

Now, stirred by resemblances in their vulnerability, young V... had applauded when public apologies were made to S... d'O....

Embittered, the insulter sought a vengeance which, anonymous this time, would be sure not to earn him a new punishment.

At an opportune moment he crept into the deserted dormitory and, apt drawing student that he was, made in charcoal on the wall behind young V...'s bed a sketch wherein, under the title "Papa's Double Blow", two hearses were seen, one behind the other, near a framed corner vignette filled by a large stamp depicting a polar catastrophe.

He began to hate his handiwork when he saw its discovery provoke a general malaise—and the tears of the concerned party.

Informed of the event, A... gathered all together—and doubly stigmatized a cowardly anonymous insult which struck at the son in the person of the father.

Then he painted such a radiant picture of redemption through confession that the miscreant, weeping in turn, came and bowed before the victim, avowing his guilt and beseeching forgiveness.

One can imagine the effect on a sister—and a twin sister at that—of a force already so dominant over mere comrades.

Each of A...'s words was an article of faith for M..., and she would gladly have braved any peril for the triumph of a cause championed by him.

And indeed, together with his inclination toward acts of goodness, the precocious adolescent did occasionally cherish great utopian dreams—which he boldly planned to realize some day.

Deeply attached as he was to his natal island, he would in particular have liked to see come into being there a more refined civilization, born out of intensive imitation of Europe.

Ardently he admired Europe, to which his Spanish blood in fact allied him: the homeland of great memories, of solid traditions, of masterpieces of art, of sublime intelligences—setting on the contrary little store by the crude industrialism of fledgling America.

And often, while confiding his thoughts to M..., he would frame passionate plans for distant future projects which this special patriotism suggested.

Alas, he was not to see that future; death which from his cradle had never ceased to hover over him took him at twenty, wasted by a malady of the lungs—under the haggard eye of M..., henceforth inconsolable.

Nonetheless, the sentiment of a sacred mission to be fulfilled sustained her in her sorrow.

A..., on his deathbed, had solemnly appointed her to realize in his stead his patriotic dream—and, with arm outstretched, she had sworn obedience.

A year later her great-aunt died full of years, leaving M... a fortune which would allow her to take up the cudgels at once.

Sensing first of all how little she would be able to accomplish alone, she had printed and circulated gratis a brochure containing an explicit call for aid. Here A...'s desideratum was fully laid out—along with the project of founding, together with those who shared her ideas, a club for both sexes whose members would meet at M...'s home.

Enthusiastic and understanding, numerous intellectuals pledged their membership with patriotic zeal.[2]

Every club must be governed; a vote was taken, and, on the first ballot, M... was unanimously elected president.

Thereupon she was urged to invent for herself some insignia, the wearing of which during meetings would attest to her authority.

Prodded thus, she began to reflect seriously and, after a period of dissatisfaction, by force of elimination finally adopted a bold idea—at first rejected as overshooting the mark.

In fact it was a matter not of a simple ornamental accessory, but of an entire costume.

Among a group of Dresden porcelains displayed from time immemorial in a vitrine in her parlour was one depicting the Rape of Europa. A graceful garment closely modelled after that of the statuette—and completed by a flesh-coloured leotard—became her presidential regalia.

The meeting at which she handselled it took on a character of inaugural solemnity. Fresh activity reigned in the search for policies to be adopted. And finally each member was given the assignment of providing appropriate testimony to Europe's superiority.

With emulation helping, it became for the intellectual elite who made up the club a race to see who would furnish the handsomest stone for the edifice.

And several weeks passed, during which M... received a sheaf of arguments for her cause: the thirty documents which follow.

—1930-31

Notes

1. Considering that Roussel has supplied names, or at any rate initials, for characters who barely make an appearance in his narrative, he seems here to be going out of his way to avoid naming the "miscreant" who plays such a pivotal role. [Trans.]

2. This sentence replaces, on the corrected proofs, the following incomplete sentence: "Numerous idlers, counting on many joyous parties purchased with little effort . . ." [Trans.]

Mardi

Cher ami

C'est entendu pour demain
mercredi 7 h.

Merci pour votre étourdissant
sonnet. Que de rimes en « roussel »
c'est un tour de force et
« tis brave » est épatant. Cela
m'a fait penser à cette rime
de douze pieds :

Dans ces meubles laqués, rideaux et dais moroses
Danse, aime, bleu laquais, rit d'oser des mots roses.

Toutes mes amitiés
Raymond Roussel

Note from Roussel, probably to Pierre Frondaie.

RAYMOND ROUSSEL
An Unpublished Note

Translation   John Ashbery

Tuesday

Dear Sir

Agreed for tomorrow Wednesday at seven.

Thank you for your astounding sonnet. So many rhymes for "Roussel"! It is a tour de force and *"lis braire"*[1] is terrific. It reminds me of this couplet of twelve-syllable lines:

> *Dans ces meubles laqués, rideaux et dais moroses*
> *Dans, aime, bleu laquais, rit d'oser des mots roses.*[2]

fondly,

Raymond Roussel

Notes

1. "read to bray", a pun on *libraire*, "bookseller". [Translator's note]
2. "Amid this lacquered furniture, these gloomy curtains and canopies,
   Dance, make love, blue lackey, laugh to venture blushing words."
   The two lines are almost identical phonetically. By an odd coincidence, Breton, who couldn't possibly have known of this letter, quotes this same couplet in his preface to Ferry's *Essay on Raymond Roussel*, attributing it to Charles Cros and citing it as a precedent for Roussel's linguistic experiments. Breton however gives *ris*, the familiar imperative of the verb *rire*, to laugh, rather than Roussel's *rit*, the third-person singular, which here makes no sense grammatically. The lines were published in an article by Charles Cros in his *Revue du Monde Nouveau* (2, April 1874), but according to the editors of the Pleiade edition of his works, are "undoubtedly not by him". They formed the first and fourth lines of a quatrain; the two inner lines are similarily constructed "totally rhyming" verses. The article satirises the formal strictures of the Parnassian poets. [Trans. note]

ALAIN ROBBE-GRILLET
Riddles and Transparencies in Raymond Roussel

Translation   Barbara Wright

Raymond Roussel describes, and beyond what he describes, there is nothing—nothing of what is traditionally called a message. To use one of the favourite expressions of academic literary criticism, Roussel doesn't seem to have "anything to say". No transcendency, no humanist "going beyond" can be imputed to the series of objects, exploits and events which from the very beginning make up his universe.

Sometimes, for the requirements of a strictly descriptive line, he tells us some psychological anecdote or metaphysical allegory, or describes some imaginary religious ritual or primitive custom . . . . But these elements never have any "content" or depth, they cannot to the slightest degree increase our knowledge of human characters or emotions or make the most modest contribution to sociology, or constitute the most insignificant philosophic meditation. It is always, in fact, a question of straightforward conventional feelings (filial love, devotion, greatness of soul, or treachery, and they are always treated in the manner of the old-fashioned print), or else of "gratuitous" rites, hackneyed symbolism or outworn philosophies. Between absolute non-sense and sense that no longer means anything, once again all that is left is things themselves, objects, actions.

Roussel is hardly more satisfying to the demands of criticism on the level of language, either. Many people have already pointed this out—to complain of it, naturally enough: Raymond Roussel writes badly. His style is flat and neutral. When he does depart from the category of the statement—the avowed platitude, that is, phrases like "there is", and "is situated at a certain distance"—it is always to fall into trivial imagery and the most hackneyed metaphors, which also come out of some arsenal of literary conventions. In fact, the organisation of the sound of his phrases, the rhythm and music of his words, seem not to present the slightest problem to the author's ear. The result is nearly all the time unattractive from the point of view of *belles lettres*: the prose varies between a stupid sort of droning and a laborious, cacophonic confusion and you have to count up the verse on your fingers to find out that the alexandrines really do have twelve feet.

So here we have the perfect reversal of what people agree to call a good writer: Raymond Roussel has nothing to say, and he says it badly . . . . And yet his books are beginning to be recognised by everyone as belonging to the most important French literature of the beginning of the century, as being among those that have exercised their fascination on several generations of writers and artists and also, without the slightest doubt, as being among those which must be considered the direct ancestors of the modern novel. Hence the continually growing interest that is now being taken in this opaque and disappointing writing.

Let us first consider its opacity. It is also an excessive transparency. As there is never anything beyond the thing described, as there is nothing supernatural hidden behind it, that is, and no symbolism (or else it's a symbolism that is immediately declared, explained and destroyed), the reader's eye is forced to fall on the surface of things: an ingenious and useless machine, a postcard of a seaside resort, a fête that develops mechanically, a demonstration of childish sorcery, etc. Such total transparency, which leaves neither shadow nor reflection behind it, in fact turns into a *trompe-d'oeil* painting. The greater the accumulation of minutiae, of details of form and dimensions, the more the object loses its depth. So this is an opacity without mystery, just as there is nothing behind the surface of a backcloth, no inside, no secret, no ulterior motive.

And yet, by one of the contradictions that occur so frequently in modern writing, mystery is one of the formal themes Roussel is fondest of using: the search for hidden treasure, the problematical origin of this or that character or of a certain object, all sorts of puzzles that his readers, as well as his heroes, are continually being faced with in the form of riddles and conundrums, of apparently absurd combinations, of key-phrases, of double-bottomed boxes, etc. Concealed exits, underground passages connecting two places with no visible link, sudden revelations about the secrets of a contested parentage, keep cropping up in this rationalistic world as in the best tradition of the detective story, and for a moment transform the geometrical space of situations and dimensions into a new *Castle in the Pyrenees* . . . . Not really, though—the mystery is all the time too well controlled. Not only are the enigmas too clearly described, too objectively analysed, and too openly stated to be enigmas, but, what is more, at the end of a speech, either long or short, their solution is disclosed and analysed, and this time with the greatest simplicity, considering the extreme complication of its various threads. After we have read the description of the baffling machine, we are treated to a detailed description of the way it works. After the riddle, we are always given its explanation, and everything is back where it was.

This is carried so far that the explanation too becomes useless. It so well answers the questions asked, it so totally exhausts the subject, that in the end it seems to be merely duplicating the function of the machine. And even when you see it working and know what it is for, it still remains bizarre—like the famous pile-driving machine used to make decorative mosaics with human teeth by harnessing the energy of the sun and wind! The effect of breaking the whole thing down to its minutest cog-wheels, and the perfect identity of these cog-wheels with the function they fulfil, is simply to bring us back to the pure spectacle of an action devoid of sense. Once again a too transparent meaning is merged in the total opacity.

Elsewhere we are at first offered a combination of the most heterogeneous possible words—placed, for instance, underneath a statue which is itself full of many disconcerting peculiarities (and described as such)—and then we are given a long explanation of the meaning (it is always *immediate*, very close to the words) of the riddle, and told how it is directly connected with the statue, whose strange details are then revealed as being absolutely necessary, etc. Now this chain of extraordinarily complex, ingenious and far-fetched elucidations seems so ludicrous and so disappointing that it is as if the mystery were still intact. But from now on it is a cleansed, eviscerated mystery that has become unnameable. The opacity no longer hides anything. We feel as if we have found a locked drawer, and then a key, and the key opens the drawer impeccably . . . and the drawer is empty.

Roussel seems himself to have been somewhat mistaken about this aspect of his work—he thought he would fill the house at the Châtelet with crowds of people dying to be present at a cascade of these—as he thought—fascinating enigmas, followed by their solution by a patient and subtle hero. Experience, alas, soon disillusioned him. It could easily have been foreseen. For he was really offering them riddles situated in a void, concrete but theoretical investigations, without anything accidental about them, and therefore not capable of trapping anyone. Yet traps are set for us on every page, but they are merely propelled in front of us, we are shown everything about the way they work, and in fact shown how not to become their victims. In any case, even if he hasn't had much experience of the way Rousselian things function and of the disappointment that must necessarily follow their fulfilment, every reader will be struck from the very beginning by the total lack of any anecdotal interest—the total pallor—in the mysteries offered us. Here again we either find a complete void, dramatically speaking, or else the world of the toy theatre, with all its conventional trappings. And in this case, whether the tales told exceed the bounds of the bewildering or not, the very way they are presented, the naivete with which the interrogations (of the order of: "Everyone present was highly intrigued by . . . ." etc.) are propounded, and finally the style, as far removed as possible from the elementary rules of suspense, would be quite enough to alienate the most sympathetic patron from these candidates for an imaginary Society of Useless Inventions in the domain of science fiction, and from these pages of folk-lore arranged like a procession of marionettes.

*

What are these forms, then, that we find so passionately interesting? And how do they work on us? What do they mean? It is still too early to answer the last two questions. The Rousselian forms haven't become academic yet, they haven't yet been digested by our culture, they haven't yet been promoted to the rank of values. What we *can* do now, though, is at least to name some of them. And to start with, there is his *experimentation*, which, in the writing, destroys its own object.

This experimentation, as we have said, is purely formal. It is primarily an itinerary, a logical path leading from a given state to another state—which is very similar to the first, even though it can only be reached by a long detour. There is another example of this, which has the additional advantage of belonging entirely to the domain of language, in the short posthumous stories whose architecture Roussel himself explained: two phrases which, to within a letter, are pronounced in exactly the same way, but whose meanings are totally unconnected, because of the different ways in which the similar words are understood. Here the distance between them is covered by the story which unites the two phrases, the first of which constitutes the first words of the text and the second the last. The most absurd episodes are thus justified through their function as utensils, vehicles, intermediaries; the story apparently has no more content, but it does have movement, order, composition—it too has become a mere mechanism; a reproducing machine and a modifying machine at the same time.

For we must insist on the importance Roussel attaches to this very slight *modification* in sound that separates the two key-phrases, not to speak of the general modification of the meaning. The story has wrought, under our very eyes, on the one hand a profound change in the meaning of the world—and of language—and on the other hand a minute and superficial displacement, (the altered letter). The text is "biting its own tail", but with a tiny irregularity, a tiny distortion . . . which alters everything.

We also frequently find simple plastic *reproduction*, like the mosaic that the previously mentioned pile-driver is designing. There are many examples of all kinds, whether in Roussel's novels, plays, or poems, of these images: statues, engravings, paintings, or even vulgar drawings with nothing in the least artistic about them. The best known of these objects is the miniature view that can be seen in the handle of a pen. Naturally, the precision of the detail is as elaborate as if the author were showing us a real, life-size scene— life-size, or even enlarged by some optical instrument, field-glasses or a micro-scope. So in a picture just a fraction of an inch long we can see a beach with several people on the sand or in small boats on the sea, and there is nothing blurred about their movements or in the contours of the scenery. On the other side of the bay is a road, and a car is being driven along this road, and a man is sitting inside the car, and the man is holding a stick, whose knob is shaped like . . . etc.

Sight, Roussel's favourite sense, very soon achieves a demented acuity, tending towards the infinite. This characteristic is probably made even more provocative in that it is a question of a reproduction. Roussel is fond of describing, as we have already pointed out, a universe which he doesn't repre-sent as real, but as already having been depicted. He likes to place an artist between himself and the world of men as an intermediary. The text we are offered is an account of the double. The inordinate enlargement of certain distant or minute elements here takes on a particular value, for the observer has not been able to go up to the detail that is attracting his attention and look at it from close to. Obviously he too is inventing, like the many creators —machines or processes—that people all Roussel's work. Sight here is *imaginary* sight.

Another striking characteristic of these images is what one might call their resemblance to *snapshots*. The wave just about to break; the child playing with its hoop on the beach; elsewhere, the statue of some eminent personage in the middle of an eloquent gesture (even if at first the meaning is missing as it is still a riddle); or an object half-way between the ground and the hand that has dropped it—everything is shown in movement by the description that leaves all gestures, falling objects, breaking waves, etc., in suspense, perpetuates the imminence of their end and deprives them of their meaning.

Empty enigmas, time standing still, signs that refuse to be significant, gigantic enlargements of minute details, tales that turn in on themselves, we are in a *flat* and *discontinuous* universe where everything refers only to itself. A universe of fixity, of repetition, of absolute clarity, which enchants and discourages the explorer . . . .

And this is where the trap once more reappears, but it is of a different nature. The clarity, the transparency, exclude the existence of other worlds behind things, and yet we discover that we can't get out of *this* world. Everything is at a standstill, everything is always happening all over again; the child is eternally holding its stick over the oblique hoop, and the foam of the motionless wave is about to fall . . . .

—1963

JEAN FERRY
Two Letters to Jacques Brunius

Translation   Antony Melville

(1965)

My dear Jacques,

It is quite natural that Breton should have copied my mistake,[1] he did not
have Roussel in front of him, he had not read it before, and I do not think he
read it afterwards. If your friend wants to prove Breton innocent he can quite
happily blame it on me. In any case, if I had not put any figures, or I had put
39, Breton would have brought in alchemy all the same, as he would if you
asked him for a preface to the telephone directory.

In fact you are right (I think my text—I do not even have a copy of it!
specifically used the word 'performance'), to get from tableau 1 to tableau 24,
the first being set up, and the last taken down *after* the performance, the
stage-hands have to perform 23 operations. Your friend is right to point out
this horrific oversight—I do hope he will say something new about Roussel;[2]
I continue to wait for something new but only ever see my work, mistaken or
otherwise, faithfully copied out. But I say again with Breton I do not feel
so odiously guilty of having set him off on a track he would have taken anyway. One only has to read Roussel (*Comment j'ai écrit...*) to realise that that
whole preface is monumental garbage. One of the most cowardly things I
have ever done was to accept it, and Leiris rightly reproached me for it at the
time. But in case your friend is a surrealist, you might point out to him that
there are 17 different sets . . . aha? . . . arcane 17??[3] That might salvage things?
—in any case, by the same post I am sending M.Heppenstall a written statement of my unworthiness . . .

Yours unfailingly as ever
Jean

★

Well, my old friend, the post isn't bad between France and England!—Your letter this morning pleased me greatly—every line strengthens the feeling of how much we have in common. Thanks!

I do not wish to start digging up the past, and to tell the truth I have forgotten the precise reasons for my separation from Breton! As the English who think they can speak French say, it was 'tout ensemble'! I had been quite exasperated by the way everyone cossetted Carrouges, and especially the little collective manifesto which went with the *Machines Célibataires*,[4] in which they were all traced back to the symbolism of the Cross! Besides which instinctively I could not stand Pauwels, for whom Breton at the time, was wild with admiration, and whom his successors are only now heaping with the insults he already deserved.[5] You know how it is with Breton, you must never be right *too early*, and in any case, not before him. But I must say that Breton personally never showed that I was out of favour other than by silence (I have not always achieved such elegance)—it was the wretched little shits that surrounded him then that barked at me so furiously. I should also say, however, that I had really had enough of sterile lyricism, and felt drawn to 'other shores', as the pseudo-Rimbauds would say, where I would not be obliged on pain of death to pass *moral* judgements on anyone!

As regards Roussel, my dear Jacques, I have always thought of you, and described you, as the last encyclopaedist, do you, yes or no, respect texts? Why do you want me to choose between Breton's poetic hypothesis and Roussel's categorical statements, the fruit of a whole life, the more uncertain of the two answers? Why should I not believe Roussel when he spells out in 'how he wrote certain of his books', where he found his situations. (I mean, his inspiration, of course!) It was not in the Cabala or any dubious initiation. You have to be reasonable—it may not be exciting—but it is probably more *moral*! Do you think Roussel, who was so proud of his *procedures*, and who drew such amazing conclusions from them, would have been pleased if he had been told that that was all wrong, and his works concealed alchemical secrets? But then, in what way would he be 'a genius with supernatural endowments'? There have been countless alchemical writings before him! And there will be plenty more! Excuse me, Jacques, but I think Roussel is *above that*! If there is any alchemy here, it is that of the word, the alchemy of the mystery of language in several stages, like rockets. The only real mystery, which psychoanalysis might find something to nibble on, is to find out *why* a particular sequence of sounds formed by words broke down for him into the particular other series which it did, and not any other. Second stage: why, starting from this second series, did he make up *these particular* stories, and not others? Might this not be because he was a poet of immense stature? I prefer to believe that the secret he had to pass on was, in his way, that of Baudelaire's Phars,[6] rather than the recipe for the philosopher's stone. One more thing one could argue about for a hundred and seven years: if the holders of the secret write, why? They do not wish to, they cannot, they must not reveal the secret! So what is the point of hiding it behind a lot of symbolism as poetic as it is impenetrable? Why? For people who would recognise the secret? But they know it already! And they must tremble to read these hints, however opaque they may be?

I am now going to reveal to you something which the surrealists would call it a crime to mention—but which proves all the same that all this is not as desperately *serious* as you seem to think. I have formal proof that Canseliet CANNOT SPEAK LATIN!!![7] So, forgive me, but for medieval symbolism, you could perhaps do better.

I am extremely interested in your new machine, and dying to see it. If you are not afraid to commit yourself, I can tell you that I plan to give up a large proportion of the next issue of *Bizarre* to a supplement or special issue. A photo of your machine would be, I am convinced, the most novel and interesting thing in the supplement. I would also be happy to feature pages by your Monsieur Heppenstall—I feel sure that if he is a friend of yours and you recommend him, and he likes Roussel—he must have written something interesting.[8] In a way he is right to attack the NIA[9] translation more than anything else. He can do word by word work which is significant, even though *demoiselle a reitre en dents* does not lead inevitably in English to the Skelderup cave—which I had such a hard time drawing!

The more I read and understand what you are saying, the more guilty I feel about Breton. What an oversight can lead to! Please explain to Heppenstall *that I did not do it on purpose.* I would not for the reasons I gave above, and even less so in order to lay a trap which Breton would inevitably run into with his head down. I do not mind being thought crazy, but I am not a bastard (at least, not to that extent!).

Having said that, are you really convinced at the deepest level that Breton, with his head stuffed with Fulcanelli, would not have found an alchemical slant to 12, 36 or no scene-changes at all? One thing is remarkable all the same. This preface was for a book which is 90% primarily about the NIA!! And he only talks about *Poussière de Soleils*! But then, what is done is done... if it was not for you, I would have died peacefully, basking in general esteem... now, I have to give up that idea!

I read your letter once again... Leiris has no more need than I to refute a hypothesis that the facts contradict with blinding clarity. And his article *Documents*... [10] come now... that was not yesterday! People change, you know... It's not a bad thing to change... You find things out...

On the same principle, I do not think Roussel was any more particularily interested in Tarots than pile-drivers, for instance, or paving machines. His tarots are either cards for playing (music!), or the phonic representation of a word like *taraud* (screw-cutter), you may be right, or several syllables, and at that level you haven't even left home yet. I will make you a present of something I have worked out. Do you know why the seeress Felicity'strains her ear' up against the Tarots which emit not only music but halos? Well I am sure it is: *'Hâlo, j'écoute?'* (Hello, who's speaking?)—Yes alright, should have thought of it—I have been stuck with correcting the proofs for the Pauvert edition—which has been neatly set from the Gallimard edition—which carried on all Rencontre's mistakes,[11] plus one or two of his own inimitable making, if I may say so. No one thought of Lemerre! (but where did Rencontre get his misprints then? A mystery).

I grasp all your excellent fingers
    your abominable Ferry

Notes

1. Breton's essay *Fronton Virage*, which prefaced Ferry's *Une Etude sur Raymond Roussel* (Arcanes, 1953) followed Ferry's mistaken assertion that there were 22 scene changes in Roussel's play *Poussière de Soleils*. Since this is the number of the arcana of the Tarot pack (and the Hebrew alphabet) Breton attributed a hermetic content to the play.
2. A hope which proved unjustified!
3. Title of a book by Breton.
4. *Les Machines célibataires*, Michel Carrouges, Arcanes, 1954.
5. Pauwels is now a prominent right-wing journalist.
6. i.e. *Les Phares* (The Lighthouses), a poem by Baudelaire from *Spleen et Ideals*. The "lighthouses" are great artistic luminaries such as Rembrandt, Rubens, etc.
7. Eugene Canseliet purports to be the pupil of the elusive alchemist Fulcanelli, however no real evidence has ever been offered to demonstrate Fulcanelli's existence, and many believe them to be one and the same person.
8. Brunius' friendship with Heppenstall was apparently somewhat short-lived. The issue of *Bizarre* (34/35, 1964) has no contribution from either author.
9. Kenneth Koch's translation of the 3rd. Canto of *Nouvelles Impressions d'Afrique* (i.e. NIA) appeared in 'Art & Literature', 2, Lausanne, 1964.
10. *Documents sur Raymond Roussel*, La Nouvelle Revue francaise, 268, 1st. Jan., 1936.

11. Ferry refers to the publishing history of *Locus Solus*. Like all Roussel's books, it was originally published, at his own expense, by the publishing house of Alphonse Lemerre (in   1914). In 1962, Rencontre (in Lausanne) reprinted the book with the permission of Roussel's estate. In 1963, Gallimard published the work, unaware that Pauvert had acquired the rights. The Pauvert edition was published in 1965.

Jean Ferry.

JEAN RICARDOU
Elocutory Disappearance

Translation   Alec Gordon

> We do not write according to what we
> are; we are according to what we
> write.
>
> *Maurice Blanchot*[1]

> Now in the red flame
> (. . .)
> Of my universal genius
> *Raymond Roussel*[2]

1. *GAMES OF THE SIMILAR*

a. *Rousselian imitation*

She, or he, who approaches this text must know that it only claims openly to
be a preface insofar as it aims to be the exact opposite, a postscript, as if the
whole text were subjected to the ineluctable turning of a wheel. This reversal
of the usual order consists, perhaps, in satisfying some penchant for pardoxes.
But it marks, above all, the concern to immediately subvert the empire of
succession through which, as we know, the domination of the linear occludes
the whole tissue of the text. Besides, what is thus laid down in filigree, by a
sort of mime, is one of the most impressive of the Rousselian gestures. To
that famous foreword in *Impressions d'Afrique* which, opening the text at
a different beginning from its true beginning, defines its reading,
tendentiously, as liable to various itineraries: "Readers who are not initiated
in the art of Raymond Roussel are advised to read this book firstly from page
217 to page 455, then from page 1 to page 211,"[3] it is possible to add—in
order to summarise our argument—the following invitation:

"Readers who are not initiated in the death of Raymond Roussel are
advised to read this book firstly from page 124 to page 146, then from page
111 to page 122."

b. *Drawing-room Impersonations*

Here we are then, doubly so, in the domain of Roussel. Not only have we taken up the strange advice but, above all, we have taken it up in strict imitations. Imitation, we are well aware, is the Rousselian operation *par excellence*. It is scarcely an accident if the penultimate paragraph of *Comment j'ai ecrit certains de mes livres*, just before Roussel registers his hope for "a little posthumous fulfilment" with regard to his texts, underlines his huge success with impersonations.

"I only really knew the feeling of success when I use to sing to my own paino accompaniment and, more especially, through numerous impersonations which I did of actors or of anyone else. But there, at least, my success was enormous and unanimous."

For Roussel, then, it was undoubtedly a question of offering these glorious imitations as the prophetic sketch, itself imitatory, of the glory to come from books composed on the principle of imitation.

2. *TEXTUAL TOPIC*

a. *Phonic topic*

Perhaps it has not been sufficiently noted: the first Rousselian procedure, working through imitation, or if one prefers, a play of similarities, is theoretically capable of manifesting itself in two domains: the phonic and the topic. With the famous coupling of the words *billard* (billiard table) and *pillard* (plunderer) it is a question of linking two words on the basis of their similar sonorities distinguished by the difference of only one of their letters. With the parody which we are proposing it is a question of linking the two words *art* (art) and *mort* (death), in spite of the difference between them, on the basis of their identical position, demonstrated by the similarity of the two sentences which accommodate them. There is, undoubtedly, a relationship of extension between the two procedures; from comparing two words we have moved on to compare two sentences. But, above all, this is a complementary relationship. The second case can, in fact, be generated from the first by a simple displacement of attention: it would then be a question of linking the two letters 'b' and 'p', in spite of the differences between them, on the basis of their identical positions, which attests to the similarity of the two words which accommodate them. Such a relationship between the phonic and the topic can be formulated according to the following theorem: when the phonic similarity between the two given verbal entities increases, it tends to define similar locations through which various phonically different elements can be linked.

b. *Metrical topic*

Certainly, the determination of a textual topic can do without the phonic topic: it is sufficient for it to have recourse to metrics. A prosaic metric which links, for example, the respective beginnings of sentences, of paragraphs, indeed of chapters and books, or their endings, or their beginnings and their endings. A poetical metric which adds the attributes of what Mallarmé called "ligne parfait" or verse, in short: the vertical relations of one ordered term to another such term.

The textual topic thus occupies at least two regions. The phonic topic determines locations where differences and similarities can be distinguished. But the positioning of similarities in these places tends to increase the basic similarity which has a tendency to imply the exact repetition of a quotation, that is, the disappearance of the problem to the benefit of various others. It is an absolute, technical limit. The metrical topic determines the locations where similarities and differences can be distinguished. But the positioning of differences in these places implies a more sensitive reading and risks not being read. It is a relative, ideological limit. There is thus no reason, therefore, in the following table, to grant perfect symmetry to the apparent crossing of the topics.

Linked Elements	Textual Topic	
	Phonic	Metrical
Similar	+ → − technical limit	+
Different	+	+ → − ideological limit

c. *Superimposition of topics*

Let us take the penultimate stanza of his poem *L'Ame de Victor Hugo* as proof that these problems are typical of Rousselian activity:

> With this explosion like
> My universal genius,
> I see the world bow down
> Before this name: Victor Hugo.

> (*A cette explosion voisine*
> *De mon génie universel,*
> *Je vois le monde s'incline*
> *Devant ce nom: Victor Hugo.*)

With a much relished lack of modesty the name of Raymond Roussel, which we have just read in filigree, ineluctably usurps that of Victor Hugo. This effect of the text arises from a mechanism in two stages: the association of the two names, and the substitution of one for the other. In order to produce the association it is theoretically sufficient to employ the metrical topic and to write another stanza of the same kind in which the two words Raymond Roussel would occupy the same place as that of Victor Hugo. Now, as we have noted, this use of different elements in a metrical device is difficult to read today. We can therefore think of overdetermining the relationship between the two locations which concern us by also activating the phonic topic. Thus the two stanzas will not only have to be of the same type; but they will have to be identical with, of course, the exception of the names of the two writers. The operation which we have accomplished above, with the parodic effect through which *art* and *death* have been linked, is no different.

The substitution implies that one will be saved having to write a stanza. Henceforth it will be a question of composing the text in such a way that the written name, in this case Victor Hugo, infringes a rule which the omitted name will obey. This law, as if by chance, is no less than the metrical topic playing on similar elements—in short, traditional rhyme.

3. ART AND DEATH

a. The initiative to words

The moment has thus come, perhaps, to give an account of the effects of the mechanics in which we have found ourselves implicated. An incident has occurred: our immediate submission to Rousselian imitation has determined the textual liason of the art and death of Raymond Roussel. Far from being dismissed as insignificant, this event must assume the most imperious emblematic value. As we have emphasised elsewhere:[4] in proportion as the number and the closeness of the connections between the signifiers of a text are increased (as we have just seen to some extent in Roussel's work), so the language tends to occupy the whole stage, whereas the author, as a subjectivity in possession of a sense, shrinks to the point of disappearing. To write is, without doubt, to put in motion the putting to death of an author. Or, in the words of Mallarme, it is even to bring about "the elocutory disappearance of the poet who concedes the initiative to words".[5]

Now since we have familiarised ourselves somewhat with the idea of the signifying space of the text, or rather with its topic, let us observe the alpha and omega of the first sentence of *Comment j'ai écrit certains de mes livres*:

"I have always intended to explain the way in which I wrote certain of my books (*Impressions d'Afrique, Locus Solus, L'Étoile au Front* and *Poussière de Soleils*)."

In its very arrangement it is already significant. If it begins with "I" the *last word* falls to "books". Pure chance? Applying to the whole surface the same law of metrical topic, let us look ahead to the last sentence of the text:

"And so I seek consolation, for want of something better, in the hope that I may perhaps gain a little posthumous fulfilment through my books."

We are then bound to admit that, apart from the conjunction, the same two elements of the lexicon figure in the same decisive locations. Further-more, over the whole of the text, the same concern evidently dictates the placing of its first and last word.

c. Biography as an effect of the text

Let us agree: the contestation of the author by his own books hardly appears to correspond, at first sight, with the extreme biographical requirements which Roussel clearly demonstrates under the pseudonym of Martial in Pierre Janet's study *Les Caractères psychologiques de l'extase:*[6]

"This glory will fall upon all my work without exception; it will illuminate all the acts of my life: all the acts of my childhood will be investigated and the way I played 'Prisoner's Base' will be admired."

But, on a closer reading of what is written, we note that far from offering the usual movement from life to text, Martial's purpose consists in writing down the opposite movement from the work towards the life. This position will moreover surprise only those who have forgotten that curious passage from *Comment j'ai ecrit...* :

"I have travelled a great deal. Notably, in 1920-1 I travelled around the world by way of India, Australia, New Zealand, the archipelagoes of the Pacific, China, Japan and America. (During this voyage I stayed for a long time in Tahiti where I rediscovered some of the characters from Pierre Loti's wonderful book.)[7] I already knew the principle countries of Europe, Egypt and all of North Africa, and later I visited Constantinople, Asia Minor and Persia. Now, from all these travels I never took anything for my books."

A significant detail: not only did Roussel not write any book based on these travels but, on the contrary, what he actually looked for in the course of one of these voyages were the characters from a book. Let us finally note that the pseudonym under which Roussel issues the biographical require-ments already stated is none other than the Christian name of a character from a book: Martial Canterel from *Locus Solus.*

c. *The acts of life*
To go further: we know that the prime Rousselian Procedure systematically employs the principle of double meaning. From the innumerable cases amassed in *Comment j'ai ecrit...* let us quote this one:

"1st *Roue* (in the sense of a car wheel) *à caoutchouc* (elastic substance— rubber); 2nd *Roue* (in the sense of a proud, swaggering person) *à caoutchouc* (rubber tree). Whence the rubber tree in Trophies Square where Talou swaggeringly plants his foot on the corpse of his enemy."

So, with regards to *Impressions d'Afrique*, it has been possible to show that "impression" might be interpreted more in the sense of "printing" than of "feeling". Now the term which Martial curiously repeats twice, as much with regards to his life as to his childhood, is not "events", nor "incidents", nor "accidents"; it is "acts": "actions" undoubtedly, but, no less certainly, "writings".[8]

It is now possible to understand that if, in his biographical notes, Roussel dwells upon his drawing-room imitations, it is because his own life is irrefutably realated to the very functioning of his books. So giving the author of *Locus Solus* a little posthumous fulfilment with regard to his books should lead us, when dealing with the acts of his death, to pay attention to anything, even to ironical excess, which manifests motives of a Rousselian order. The first word of the title, fortunately selected by Leonardo Sciascia, is far from diverting us from this track.

4. ROUSSELIAN THANATOGRAPHY

a. *Repetitions*

Offering the widest extension to the principle on which his own surname is constructed (will a systematic survey ever be conducted on the ways in which a text works on the name which signs it: that Bauderlairian "Albatross", for example, "prince of the clouds", which derives from a Rousselian reading of *"beau de l'air"*?),[9] Sciascia evidently takes pleasure in staging, with a stream of testimonies, a whole litany of repetitions. And this information, amassed in large quantities, far from increasing our certainty about Roussel's death, gradually combines to make the event problematic: is this alleged suicide an accident? Is this alleged accident a suicide? Could it be something else again? From one testimony to another a corpus with slight variations is gradually formulated weaving a surreptitious network of tiny uncertainties. So what we see being brought into play, by this means, is Rousselian repetition itself. Not so much, undoubtedly, the kind of repetition which is multiplied in the stories by all kinds of mechanisms, various reproductions or cyclical tales, but the sort of productive repetition, shown earlier by which the link between the signifiers is expressed, often with only a slight difference, as in *billard-pillard.*

b. *Sexuality as symbol*

Now, this repeating with slight variation which Roussel rightly associates with rhyme, no doubt causes a perfect scandal. A proverb undertakes to inform us: rhyme is not reason (*rime n'est pas raison*). When any two signifiers find themselves linked by rhyme there is, in effect, double subversion: on the one hand, the alleged pure thought is perturbed by the legible efficacy of the language; on the other, a curious mixture of the heteros (on the level of the signifieds) is unquestionably displayed. It would not be contrary to our undertaking to note that the two allegations in the text in question curiously present, like a symbol of Rousselian productive rhyme, their contradiction about the sexuality of Raymond Roussel. One policeman, affirming that the housekeeper is a mistress, believes Roussel to be heterosexual; homosexuality is postulated by the chauffeur as he prepares the way for blackmail.

c. *Names and numbers*

To go further, as Sciascia opportunely points out, signifiers intervene in Roussel's 'Acts' with surprising frequency. The name of his housekeeper, Dufrêne, appears as an inversion of Fredez, Dez-fre, linked with a variation which makes it sound French; inversely, the Christian name of Charlotte is Italianised into Carlotta. Later Fredez recurs, repeated as "Freder", which differs precisely by one letter. The name of the mother, Chaslon, becomes Chalon. The author of *Locus Solus* is named as Armand, his approximate anagram. Variant for variant let us note that a similar Christian name might have permitted the supreme irony of attributing *Locus Solus* to another author of the time: Romain Roussel.[10] As for the instrument which plays an important role, the "Gillette" razor, does it not, in the Rousselian manner become "Gilet"?[11]

Elsewhere,[12] we supposed that one of Roussel's stories, *Parmi les Noirs* (Among the Blacks), in which there are many numerical references, appeared to be a text of numbers, or rather, a numbered text. After this how can we fail to emphasise this same feature of the text written at Roussel's request— the housekeeper's diary which refers to his last days:

"The diary of Madame Fredez-Dufrêne, that is the page which has been attached to the 'Acts', begins on Sunday 25th June. That evening, at six o'clock, Roussel took 6 Phandorme tablets, then again, the same number at half past one in the morning. On the 26th he began at ten past five in the afternoon with 8 Hipalene; he took two more of these and immediately after that 4 more at half past nine; 30 others 'in all during the night'."

And how can we fail to hypothesis that, apart from recording terrible technical details, this text demonstrates the use of an underlying Rousselian numbering system?

d. *The legible island* (L'ile lisible)

Admittedly, to penetrate into the scandalous domain where words take the initiative is, perhaps, to discover a certain logic in a mass of apparently fortuitous events. The island: we know Roussel's aptitude for deriving, through rhyme, further words from one word and we have not forgotten that he wishes to see "the world bow down before" his name. Roussel, therefore, is *roue* (wheel) and *sel* (salt). As Sciascia points out, the place chosen for the improbable mildness of its climate in summer offers the invaluable advantage of being a maritime island: an area entirely subjected to a salt (*sel*) environment. And what does his only activity in all these last days amount to? Travelling indefinitely around this region with his chauffeur in a vehicle with wheels (*à roues*).

But, for such a wealthy traveller who has covered the globe, islands set in seas are innumerable. So why, precisely, should he have chosen the Mediterranean? As its name makes obvious this sea is set within surrounding landmasses. Now it is scarcely a question of just any continent: of the two novels by Roussel one, *Impressions* is supposed to take place in Africa and the other, *Locus Solus*, in Europe, not far from Paris. Enclosed in this way the Mediterranean is pre-eminently suitable as a sea welcoming Roussel between two of his books.

But between Europe and Africa there are still numerous insular solutions. Why, then, Sicily? Let us look more closely at the map: there is surely no other island than this one between Tunisia and Italy which is better able to mark the half-way situation. What is more, does not such an island, distinguished by a volcano, offer the very site, fire and sea, in which Rousselian production is accomplished throughout the lines of *L'Ame de Victor Hugo*:

> My soul is a strange factory
> Where fire and the waters are in conflict . . .
>
> (*Mon âme est étrange usine*
> *Où se battent le feu, les eaux . . .*)

But there is still an abundance of islands between Italy and Tunisia dominated by a volcano. So why precisely this island? Let us re-read, in this connection Sciascia's text. Roussel had already undergone two detoxification cures: the first in Switzerland, the second "near Paris". Now, unremittingly, the excessive use of barbiturates has taken hold of him again. Treatment thus becomes necessary and he eventually agrees to the idea of another stay in Switzerland. From that moment on everything happens as if Roussel's acts form a series of simulacra strangely following an exact Rousselian procedure. Between the action to be accomplished and the substitute action to which it is limited many similarities are brought into play, affecting particularly the signifiers. Roussel will have to go to Switzerland. Now in one sense Switzerland is an island surrounded by land. Choosing an island surrounded by sea is therefore symbolic, a way of going there. And it is not just any Mediterranean island which is chosen but the very one whose name, Sicily (*Sicile*), has the same number of letters in French as Switzerland (*Suisse*) and which, furthermore, begins and ends in the same way.

e. *Rousselian poligraphy*

Let us suppose we have a sceptical reader: he is determined to question our reasoning. Abandoning geography and soon taking refuge in the town, he presents arguments which will lead to what, indulging in a word-play not too ill-timed, we will call Rousselian poligraphy (without a 'y'). First of all points out that the decision to return to Switzerland was taken in Sicily and, from what we know, this return might therefore just as easily have been planned for "near Paris". To be perfectly rigorous, it would have been necessary to satisfy the analogy with Paris as well as with Switzerland. He next asks why that town and not another? Why that hotel and not another one? And as for the chauffeur—why was he in another hotel? And why that particular one?

Excessive as these questions may be, they can be answered very precisely. The choice of Palermo, as we have seen, not only permits a substitute for Switzerland but also, as we shall see, a substitute for Paris. Like Paris Palermo is a capital, also like Paris Palermo begins with the letters P and a.

As for the *Grand Hôtel des Palmes*: who, now, could remain blind to the reasons for his choice? Is not the palm the emblem of that glorious victory with which Roussel, who thought himself Napoleon's equal, everywhere appeared to be pathologically obsessed? Could the epithet "Grand" contribute to reduce its allurements? And who could fail to see that it is very nearly a rhyme which links the name Palermo to Palmes?

f. *O Death, where are your words?*[13]

It becomes possible for us, then, to understand the end. Roussel moves inside Rousselian simulacra. He has now promised to return to Switzerland: each day, on each drive, he goes there. Because of this he has taken the trouble to install his chauffeur in a very special place: the Savoia hotel—in French "*Savoie*". The chauffeur who takes him out each day is therefore staying at a hotel whose name not only represents a region bordering on Switzerland (*Suisse*); it is also made up of the same number of letters and begins and ends in the same way (*Savoie=Suisse*).

It is now night and departure is imminent. The sick man pushes paradox to its limits: he wishes for a cure, but his desire is to ingest more barbiturates. Accepting the journey, he mimes it by shifting his mattress; rejecting it, he takes more Soneryl. Accepting the journey, his face is turned towards the connecting door; rejecting it, he has closed that same door.

What the character must now perform for this story to reach its proper end is an act in both the senses of action and the written word. A word capable of encapsulating in its sonorities both the site of the clinic, Switzerland, and the site of the drugs, Sicily. A word capable of allowing a final lingering doubt, by the timely difference of one letter, about the nature of the incident, suicide or not. Finally a word conforming, appropriately, in the number of letters, to the seven letters of the glorious name Roussel. Accustomed as we have become to these inadmissable procedures, we have long since guessed the emblem of this elocutory disappearance:

SUICILE

—1972

Notes

1. From *L'Espace Littéraire*, Gallimard, 1955, p. 88. [Translator's note]
2. From *L'Ame de Victor Hugo*, part II, p.63 & part II, p.171. The original French reads: *A present dans la flamme rousse / (. . .) / De mon génie universel.* The word play on the line endings—*rousse* and univers*el*- is impossible to render into English because of the change in word order required by the translation. [Translator's note]
3. The famous foreword (green advice label) referred to here was pasted across the head of the full text of *Impressions d'Afrique* published in 1932 (p.9).
   The equivalent starting number in the Pauvert edition of 1963 is p.147 and in the English translation (1966) p.152. [Translator's note]
4. In *L'Activité rousselliene*, in *Tel Quel*, No. 39, 1969, pp.78-99. Republished in *Pour une théorie du Nouveau Roman*, Editions du Seuil, 1971, pp.91-117. [Author's note]
5. From "Variations on a Subject".
6. Martial was the name Janet gave to Roussel when he published this case study. Roussel reprinted it in *Commet j'ai écrit...*, and to that extent acknowledged some degree of 'authorship'.
7. The book Roussel refers to is *Le Mariage de Loti*, first called "Rarahu", published in 1880. After Jules Verne and Victor Hugo, Pierre Loti (1850-1923) was Roussel's favourite writer. Roussel says he met the originals of some of the characters in *Le Mariage de Loti* first published 40 years before, which describes a period eight years earlier still. [Translator's note]
8. 'Acts': As Ricardou points out in the next paragraph, Sciascia chose this word for the title of his essay quite deliberately. In Italian *atti* and in French *acte* have the double meaning of an 'action' and a 'document'. Perhaps the nearest, but still unsatisfactory, equivalent in English is 'deed'. The word has been translated here, and in the next essay, as 'act' and is given in single inverted commas. [Translator's note]
9. As noted by a writer with an ornithological surname: Michel Butor (bittern). [Author's note]
10. Romain Roussel (1898-1973), French novelist and journalist.
11. 'Gilet': waistcoat.
12. In Jean Ricardou, op. cit., p.87. The section *Je suis un texte chiffre* (I am a numbered text). [Author's note]
13. The French reads: *O mort, ou sont tes mots?* To repeat the last sentence of the previous paragraph with the due substitutions: ". . . who could fail to see that it is very nearly a rhyme which links the words *Mort* and *mot*. [Translator's note]

Raymond Roussel and Charlotte Dufrène in 1911.

LEONARDO SCIASCIA
Acts Relative to the Death of Raymond Roussel[1]

Translation   Alec Gordon

"Police Station of the State Police—Politeama Sect.—Palermo 14th July 1933
Year XI of the Fascist Era
Internal Telegram
Illustrisimo Signor Primo Pretore
Illustrissimo Signor Questore
Palermo"

"This morning at about ten o'clock Antonio Kreuz, floor-porter at the Hôtel des Palmes, went to room no. 224 occupied by Raymond Roussel, a French citizen, born in Paris on the 20-1-1877. He noted that the aforesaid was lying dead on a mattress placed directly on the floor. Roussel, as we later learned, was sick in the brain, and took medicines to dull his senses. On his bedside table we found two tubes of 'Sonneril'; furthermore, the drawers of the wardrobe contained a great quantity of all sorts of medicines. We conclude that the subject caused his own death by taking an excessive dose of these medicines. The body of Roussel is under police supervision, awaiting Your visit. Subject to further enquiries."

Doctor Michele Margiotta, Magistrate of the IVth section, went to the Hôtel des Palmes[2], via Ingham, second floor, room 224, where the corpse lay of the person "whose death can be considered an offence". He pointed out, "in the first place that, on a mattress placed directly on the floor, the corpse of a man apparently — years old is lying on his back"; and, "in the second place that, the abovementioned corpse is dressed as follows: white night-shirt, white underpants, black socks and a champagne-coloured vest of fine wool". (Champagne, for the colour of the vest is not a caprice of the Magistrate, it was then in fashion.)

Doctor Federico Rabboni was present in room 224 as an expert; also present were the floor-porters Antonio Kreuz, 37 years old, son of Antonio Kreuz, of Vienna and Loi Antonio, 30 years old, son of the late Guiseppe Antonio, of Cagliari; these two, when requested "carefully to examine the corpse and to state to whom it had belonged 'in life', replied one after the other in the following terms: the corpse shown to me by Your Excellency is that of Raymond Roussell (sic), born in Paris on the 20-1-1877, son of the late   and of the late Marguerite Chalon[3]". The mother's name, the place and date of birth, which the floor-porters certainly did not know, were subsequently recorded in the police report by a different pen. The father's name was not mentioned: one of those oversights, those lapses, those mistakes which border on the mysterious, on the unfathomable; and if Savinio had found himself faced with these papers, he would have been delighted.

After identification by the porters, the Magistrate had "the above-mentioned corpse undressed according to the provisions of the law". Doctor Rabboni proceeded to the external examination and declared: "this is a man of ormal type (sic: normal type), well-developed musculature and fatty tissue, a state of semi rigor mortis, skin colour particularily pale—Hypostatic blotches on the back and lower limbs. No external lesion is noted, except for an abrasion of the epidermis of the left hemi-thorax, not of recent date—and, except for a discontinuity on the lower third of the left forearm, affecting the outer integument for two centimetres—and having the characteristics of a lacerated-contused wound of fairly recent date. The wound in question is protected by a dressing of gauze and cotton-wool spread with ointment.

Concluding his examination Doctor Rabboni dictated: "Considering the the abovementioned Roussel died a natural death, probably caused by poisoning due to the narcotics and sleeping tablets found in great quantity in his room, I consider an autopsy to be unnecessary". At the request of the Magistrate, he specified: "Death occurred approximately ten or twelve hours ago. I rule out the idea that death might have been due to the excoriations revealed on the left hemi-thorax or to the lesions on the lower third of the left forearm. I also rule out the idea that death might have been due to a violent factor."

Attached to this "official report" is a bill of expenses for "handling corpse Roussel Raymond": 10 lire. The remuneration of the medical expert—15.28 lire—on the other hand, is marked on the upper edge of the first page.

The Magistrate then dictated a "report of summary enquiries": he described the dead man once more, this time reckoning his apparent age as fifty years old but overlooking the champagne-coloured vest; and he began to describe and make an inventory of everything which was in the room. Two small separate beds, one of them intact and the other one without its mattress "which, as we said before, is on the floor and upon which the abovementioned man is lying dead." "Under the mattress is a chamber-pot containing a small amount of urine": under the mattress placed on the floor, which is curious. In any case, the detail serves, we believe, to place the time of death at a late hour of the night. At the foot of a small unmade bed a small table with four bottles of Fiuggi water and two small empty tubes of Soneryl, of twenty tablets each and each tablet of ten centigrams: and he deduced from this that Roussel had swallowed all forty of them the previous evening; which does not mean, as we shall see, that he intended to kill himself.

In the drawer of a bed-side table were found 16 bottles of Somnothyril, 15 bottles of Soneryl, 10 of Hypalene, 11 of Rutonal, 8 of Phano-dorme, one box of Declonol, one small bottle of Hyrpholene and a small tube of Somnothyril; and in a large cardboard box, in the wardrobe, 10 bottles of Neurinase and 12 of Veriane. On top of the wardrobe, half-empty bottles of Veriane, Veronidin, Neurinase and Neosedan. In the drawer of a small table, a thermometer and a light blue sheet of paper on which had been noted the barbiturates taken by Roussel from the 25th June to the 13th July, the doses, the times and the reactions. The sheet was removed as evidence and added to the 'acts'.

Rummaging in the drawers, they find two letters, one signed Cassiffari (?), the other signed Malet; and analyses of glycemia, azotemia and urine. In the wardrobes and scattered in the room, clothes and under-linen. A large suitcase and a small one for necessities. A polished silver watch. Two hats. "Twelve uncut volumes entitled *Locus Solus* by Armand Roussel." This abstracted-ness on the part of the clerk of the Magistrate's Court (illegible signature) astounds us even more than the stars in the sky. Where did he find the name Armand? Was this not the greatest twist of fate for Roussel, who had desparately sought glory? Twelve uncut copies of *Locus Solus*: a book written by another man, according to the clerk, and not by this dead man in the white night-shirt and black socks being handled by undertakers. (Curious detail: there were thirteen uncut copies one of which Roussel had offered the previous day to Professor Michele Lombardo, the hotel doctor, recommending that he begin reading at page thirty-three.[4] "What comes before is useless." That calls to mind Campana, when he sold the *Conti orfici* in cafés: after examining the face of the purchaser he used to tear out the pages which he thought to be "useless"; there were even certain people to whom he only gave the cover. But as for the first thirty-three pages of *Locus Solus*, as well as the first nine chapters of the *Impressions d'Afrique*, Roussel did not call them "useless" in that sense: it was a question of the very game and mystery of his writing. He also made Professor Lombardo a present of the third edition of *Impressions d'Afrique*, with the green 'advice' slip: "Readers who are not initiated in the art of Raymond Roussel are advised to read this book firstly from page 217 to page 455, then from page 1 to page 211".[5]

"In the room no disorder is noted which might indicate a fight . . . Nothing abnormal . . . The bedroom connects with a bathroom, where there is some dirty linen and a wardrobe containing women's clothes. The door connecting with the next room occupied by Madame Fredez is closed on the inside and the key is left in the lock. Just behind the door is the mattress on which the dead body of Roussel lies. In the suitcase different papers of patrimonial interest are found, as well as eleven fifty lire notes in the jacket hanging from the coat-stand." The money is put in the suitcase and the suitcase is sealed. A trunk standing in the corridor is brought into the room. Two strips of white cloth are stuck with four pads of lacquered wax to the door connecting with room 226. The Magistrate then passes on to the cross-examination of witnesses. The floor-porter Kreuz is called once again and declares: "I had been serving Monsieur Roussel for about one month; he lived with a lady who occupies the adjoining room number 226. I consider that Monsieur Roussel and the lady were on very good terms, for I never heard any arguments. In Monsieur Roussel's room I always noticed small bottles of medicines, but I do not know what he used them for. I often found the empty bottles in the waste-bin." He is followed by the waiter Tommaso Orlando di Gaetano, 29 years old, from Salerno: "I had been serving Monsieur Roussel for about one month; he lived with a lady who still occupies the adjoining room, number 226. I often served lunch and breakfast in their rooms; they used to take lunch together. However, in the evening, only the lady dined; Monsieur Roussel only ate one meal. I consider that these two people lived in complete harmony for I never noted any quarrels or arguments. I had noticed that there were always numerous bottles of medicines in Monsieur Roussel's room and I do not know what he used them for."[6]

Leopoldo Serena, Manager of the hotel, 42 years old, born at Capri, son of the late Federico Serena, declares: "About forty days ago, Monsieur Roussel, accompanied by Madame Fredez, booked in at the hotel which I manage. Monsieur Roussel seemed to be unwell and from the very first day he stayed in his room where he even took his meals. After a few days Madame Fredez left for Paris to pick up some luggage saying that signor Roussel found our climate to his taste and intended to stay a long time in Palermo. The day following the lady's departure, the service staff came and reported to me that

Monsieur Roussel had lost consciousness and was lying beside his bed. That happened about one month ago. I called Professor Lombardo, the hotel doctor, who looked after the patient. A few days later, Madame Fredez returned to Palermo; she found Monsieur Roussel quite well recovered. Several days later the service staff informed me that Monsieur Roussel had injured himself while he was in the bathroom. For yet a second time Professor Lombardo was called. Finally, this morning, I was informed that Monsieur Roussel was lying unconscious in his room on a mattress placed on the floor. Professor Lombardo, who was at the hotel, certified the death. Monsieur Roussel had left no deposit at the hotel. On the other hand, Madame Fredez, who dealt with payments, had deposited 25,000 francs. She withdrew 15,000 francs leaving free disposal of the rest for the funeral and possible expenses."[7]

Professor Michele Lombardo, who was thirty-seven years old thirty-seven years ago, an inhabitant of Palermo, finds himself in a somewhat delicate situation: he has not declared Roussel's suicide attempt. But in this first interrogation the Magistrate does not challenge him about such an omission. "About thirty days ago I was informed that there was a gentleman at the Grand Hôtel who was feeling ill. I hurried along and examined him. I learned later that his name was Roussel Raymond. I found him completely unconscious. From the examination carried out on the patient and from the medicines which I found in the room (Veronal, Neurinase and others) I understood that I was dealing with a subject affected by poisoning due to barbiturates. Such medicines produce euphoria (state of drunkeness). I performed a blood-letting and gave him a glucose hypodermic injection in order to check the poisoning. I also carried out catheterisations of the ureter in order to empty the urinary bladder. I also used a clyster for the same purpose. A rapid improvement was obtained and he was completely better within two days. A few days later Madame Fredez (*Professor Lombardo had dictated 'Madame Dufrène': but the name was, as they say in bureaucratic Italian jargon,* 'carcerato' *[incarcerated], that is to say, circumscribed in a rectangle*[8]), who meanwhile had returned from France and was living with Monsieur Roussel, informed me that the latter had for more than two years been taking various preparations containing barbiturate substances. She added that it had been impossible to prevail upon him to limit his use of these preparations, for he then became irascible. After a few days I was called once more. During a nervous attack in the bathroom the said Roussel had inflicted on himself superficial lesions all over his body and one more serious lesion on his left wrist from which he had lost a lot of blood. I dressed his wounds and stitched the one on his wrist. While the lesions found on different parts of the body healed rapidly, because they were very superficial, the wrist wound, which was deeper, was slow to heal and needed further treatment.

At the request of the Magistrate he replies (initialled WR, 'witness replies', which we will also use): "Monsieur Roussel was in an habitual state of intoxication because he used to take heavy doses of drugs every day. I have been able to establish this, particularily these last days, in the course of my treatment of his wrist-wound." WR: "In my capacity as a doctor I have tried more than once to urge him to stop his abuse of drugs, but Roussel always replied that this was not possible. During the last days, on my advice and on that of Madame Fredez Carlotta (*two 'incarcerations'* [carcerazioni] *this time; and there must have been debate between the doctor and the Magistrate on the lady's name. The clerk had written Fredez, then he had crossed it out and replaced it with Dufrène, then having 'incarcerated' Dufrène he had returned to Fredez*), he had decided to leave for a sanatorium in Switzerland for a cure for his addiction. It seems, however, that Monsieur Roussel was seeking to postpone his departure, perhaps because he wanted to continue his abuse of drugs."

It is the turn of madame (it is written thus in the report) Charlotte Fredez, 53 years old, daughter of the late Charles Fredez and the late Alfonsina Acard, from Paris, living at number 47 rue Pierre Charon, 8th. district. WR: "I had been co-habiting with Monsieur Raymond Roussel for about 23 years, although I was not married to him. He has always been neurasthenic. He was very involved with literature and music; he has written plays and composed music. In France he was considered a genius. He belonged to an influential Parisian family—his sister had married the Duc d'Elchingen. I know that the deceased, Monsieur Roussel, has deposited his last will and testament with the notary Constantin,[9] No. 9 rue Boissy d'Anglais, Paris." WR: "For more than two years, in order to relieve his neurasthenia, Monsieur Roussel had been taking various medicines which afforded him a feeling of well-being. So that, little by little, he had been poisoning himself. He went twice to a sanatorium, to Valmont in Switzerland for one month and a second time, for eight months, to Saint-Cloud near Paris, to a clinic at 2, Avenue Pozzo di Borgo, run by Professor Saulier, to treat his neurasthenia—but instead of leaving cured he continued to feel unwell and began to find relief in drugs which were, however, gradually poisoning him. About 40 days ago we had come to Palermo attracted by the mild climate. Since he had found the stay in Palermo to his taste I returned to Paris to collect the things necessary for a long stay. When I returned I learned that Monsieur Roussel had been ill, that

Dimanche 25 Juin. 6h soir 6 phanodorme 6 vers 1h½ matin
Lundi 26. — 8 Hypalène à 5h10 - puis 2 Th à 9h½ et 30 en tout dans la nuit
Mardi 27 — 1 bouteille ½ Vériane
Mercredi 28 — 3 Rutonal à 4h7½ - 3 à 6 heures
Jeudi 29 — 4 Soneryl à 18 en tout dans sommeil (3h. à 5 heures - 4 à 6h½ sommeil à
Vendredi 30 — Somnothyril 19 sans euphorie - sommeil 6h en 10h. et 13 dans la nuit - dormi 12h½ euphorie extra. 24h
Samedi 1er Juillet 1 bouteille Neurinase
Dimanche 2 — 1 tout Actia
Lundi 3 — 10 phanodorme et H.C. nouv méd.
Mardi 4 — Vériane 1 bout ½ et ½ Neurinase
Mercredi 5 — 2 bouteilles Véronidia
Jeudi 6 — Soneryl 16 - sommeil 9h½ euphorie grand
Vendredi 7 — Hypalène 9h soir - 6 - 18 et 3 Soneryl
Samedi 8 — 20 Somnothyril - 1 bout Neurinase pas déjeuné euphorie toute la journée
Dimanche 9 — 11 phanodorme
Lundi 10 — Véronidia 9 heures 2 bout - bon sommeil
Mardi 11 — Rutonal 9h. = 84 - 8h sommeil
Mercredi 12 — Vériane. 1 bouteille ½ formidable euphorie sommeil euphorie
Jeudi 13 — Soneryl insomnie
Vendredi 14 —
Samedi 15 —   le peu est si grand. Je pars
                               S. Charlotte Fredez
Dimanche 16 —   Palerme 14/7/1933
Lundi 17 —
Mardi 18 —
Mercredi 19 —
Jeudi 20 —

Madame Fredez's "Diary".

he had been found unconscious as a result of an overdose of narcotics, that is why I tried to convince him to leave and to go to a sanatorium. My prayers remained unanswered when I urged him at least to reduce his use of narcotics." WR: "For about ten days, so as not to be disturbed during the night, he had taken care to close the connecting door between his room and mine, leaving open the door onto the corridor. On the 2nd. of this month, perhaps while under the influence of the drugs, when he was in the bathroom he inflicted lesions on different parts of his body and on his wrist with a razor, that is why Doctor Lombardo was called urgently; who was already treating him for the wound on his wrist. From that moment, I was careful to lock up the razors to avoid his hurting himself again. These last days, on my entreaty and on the advice of Doctor Lombardo, he had decided to enter a sanatorium in Switzerland and we were ready to leave the day after tomorrow. This morning I learned through the service staff that Monsieur Roussel was lying unconscious." When he later heard the floor-porter Kreuz for the third time the Magistrate contested this point but only to eliminate from the 'acts' the contradiction between the two versions. The correction to Madame Fredez's statement was evidently added later: "I mean: I entered the room at the same time as the floor-porter." The testimony of the lady continues: "On the wish of Monsieur Roussel I kept a diary of the special medicines which he swallowed daily—a diary which he kept to hand so as to alternate the drugs. Here are the entries for the last days." WR: "In the 23 years we lived together I never had any quarrels with Monsieur Roussel. I always intervened for his own good, imploring him to restrict his use of these drugs—but in order to avoid outbursts of temper I had to leave him alone." WR: "The medicines he took made him euphoric and then he could speak for a long time without becoming tired, at other times on the other hand, they depressed him. Yesterday evening he had seemed to me stranger than usual—I asked him if he had taken a heavy dose of drugs and he answered, bluntly, 'No.' Yesterday evening at 22.15 hours, I retired to my room and Monsieur Roussel stayed in his, closing the connecting door. At about 23.00, through the closed door, I asked him how he was and he answered irritably: 'Don't worry yourself.'

The lady must have heard something to make her think Roussel was still awake: the noise of the mattress being taken off the small bed and dragged between the connecting door and the balcony; the pouring of water into the glass, certainly more than once, for him to swallow all those Soneryl tablets. His abrupt way of replying gives the impression anyway that the barbiturate had not yet had any effect. The lady knew that he was to take Soneryl that evening and had noted it in the diary, but Roussel had waited for her to retire before swallowing the medicine. Judging by the effects mentioned in the diary it must have been his favourite barbiturate: that evening, in order perhaps to die, more probably in order to fall asleep quickly and then reach a state of euphoria, he had decided to take a high, but not extraordinarily high, dose of the drug.[10]

The diary of Madame Fredez-Dufrène, that is , the page which has been atttached to the 'acts' begins on Sunday 25th. June. That evening, at six o'clock, Roussel took 6 Phanodorme tablets, then again, the same number at half past one in the morning. On the 26th., he began at ten past five in the afternoon with 8 Hipalene; he took two more of these and immediately after that 4 more at half past nine; 30 others "in all during the night". The 27th: one and a half bottles of Veriane. The 28th: at sixteen-thirty hours, 3 Rutonal tablets, three more at eighteen hundred hours, twelve more during the night: "18 in all without sleep"; or rather, with three hours sleep. The 29th. is the great Soneryl day: 4 at seventeen hundred hours, 4 at eighteen-thirty hours; sleep at twenty-two hundred hours. During the night, 13 more. After a sleep of twelve and a quarter hours, "wonderful euphoria" for twenty-four hours. The 30th: "Somnothyril 19 without euphoria", but with six hours sleep. The 1st. July: one bottle of Neurinase. The 5th: two bottles of Veronidin. The 6th: he returns to Soneryl: 16 tablets, nine and a half hours sleep, "very great euphoria". The 7th: at half past nine in the evening, 6 Hypalene, then 18, then 3 Soneryl; "a good state of euphoria". The 8th: 20 Somnothyril tablets and a bottle of Neurinase: without eating, but in a state of euphoria all day. The 9th: 11 Phanodorme tablets. The 10th: two bottles of Veronidin at twenty-one hundred hours; a good sleep. The 11th, at the same time: 34 Rutonal tablets; three hours sleep and then "marvellous euphoria". The 12th: one and a half bottles of Veriane; a little sleep and then "excessive euphoria". Thursday, 13th, the last note: Soneryl. The fact that he returned to Soneryl, the barbiturate which—from what can be deduced from the diary—afforded him a long sleep followed by extraordinary euphoria, makes us believe that he did not wish to die. Even while allowing that he took the entire contents of the two small tubes, that is, 40 tablets (one of the two might not have been entirely full), we cannot believe that he foresaw their fatal effect nor, in short, that he took them with the express intention of dying. On the 26th, in the course of the evening and night, he had taken 44 Hypalene tablets; on the 11th. July, 34 Rutonal tablets, at once. If he had wanted to commit suicide, he would have taken a higher dose than ever before. Furthermore, it is fairly improbable that a drug-addict, even in his moments of "normality", might consider his drug as a possible cause of death or would believe that an exceptional increase in dosage would fail to give him an exceptional state of euphoria. We have proof of this with Roussel's suicide attempt in the bath, by cutting the veins of his wrist. This was the second time he had tried this method of killing himself. He had noted —as he said after the first time—how easy and pleasant it is to die in this way. He only had to tear off the dressing on his wrist and he would have slipped easily and pleasantly into death.

But, that evening, Roussel did not wish to die; we believe he simply wanted to sleep. He was relying on Soneryl, which two weeks before had afforded him a sleep of twelve and a quarter hours. Certainly, for about ten days he had been more sombre and irascible than usual. Having tried (rather than attempted) to die, he had reluctantly promised to enter a clinic to undergo detoxification. From that moment, his companion—who lately had added a sort of complicity to her submissiveness with the diary she kept for him, recording the doses and their effects—had become the witness and guardian of this promise (for him so terrible) to cut himself off from drugs. An enemy. Consequently, for about ten days, from the 2nd, to be exact, he had locked the connecting door; and it is certain that he spent the nocturnal solitude which this gained for him thinking out a number of excuses and subterfuges to delay his departure or even to forget his promise. And then, the fact that he appeared "stranger than usual" that evening to Madame Fredez is understandable. He had scarcely two days of freedom left; his delirious longing to back out of his promise must have been desperate. The little sleep he had had the night before, his excessive state of euphoria, his obsession with that promise which he did not wish to keep; and, besides that, the uproar—voices, noises, explosions—of a festival. Moreover, a double festival, both patriotic and religious, since the annual 'feast day' in honour of Santa Rosalia coincided with an event which was cause for rejoicing throughout the whole of Italy. That day, Balbo's air squadron, the 'Atlantic' squadron, had arrived at Cartwright, in Labrador. The authorities had ordered a "great popular demonstration" to begin spontaneously at 19.00 hours. Roussel had gone out that afternoon, as usual: for, contrary to the legend concerning his travelling habits—in his sumptuous, funereal 'roulotte' from a hotel in one town to one in another—in Palermo, from what Gaetano Orlando remembers, he used to go out nearly every day. He had a car with a chauffeur, the chauffeur was staying in another hotel, the Savoia, and was ready punctually in front of the Hôtel des Palmes when Roussel came down to go out. But it is not known where he used to go; what is certain is that he knew no-one in Palermo: perhaps he had himself driven around town at random without ever alighting from the car, for he had difficulty in walking. Precisely that evening, on his return, he was no longer able to stand upright. He was carried from the car to the lift and then from the lift to his room by the chauffeur and the waiter Orlando. He was exhausted. But he did not forget to give Orlando his usual tip, as he did every evening: a "silver coin" (*'pataconne' d'argento*) worth twenty lire, recalls Orlando, the one with the profile of Mussolini and the fasces of a lictor. Only one evening, the 1st. July, Orlando received a hundred franc note instead of the usual "coin": but, for this, Roussel required a supplementary service. He entrusted him with the razor and then, without speaking, he made him understand, through gestures, that he wanted Orlando to cut him across the veins of his wrist. Orlando was alarmed; he said: "no, no, Monsieur Roussel"; he wanted to return the hundred francs. Roussel refused and took back the razor and the following morning he did it himself.[11]

But let us come back to the evening of the 13th. Roussel returned to the hotel when the demonstration had already started, presumably in the Piazza Castelnuovo, where gatherings and meetings always take place amidst shouting and speeches. A few steps away from the Hôtel des Palmes. More bizarre than usual, the bad mood caused by his having to leave for the sanatorium was aggravated by the mood which the "vile, municipal, dense crowd is capable of provoking in a man such as he" (we quote, not by chance, the *Sonetto autunnale al marchese di Brandomín:* by Darío for Valle-Inclán), and, more unsteady than usual, he finally reached the reassuring walls of room number 224. However, it looked onto the via Mariano Stabile,[12] which that evening must have been a torrent of sound. Having taken part in the Fascist demonstration, the crowd rushed to the festival in honour of Santa Rosalia. In the programme at 21.30 hours, there was to be a "competition of fantastic, allegorical lights on boats and barges on the stretch of water in front of the Foro Umbert"; and immediately afterwards, at 22.00 hours, another competition was scheduled: one of those infernal, pyrotechnic competions which mark the end of Sicilian religious festivals and which are judged not only by the fantasy of the design and colours of the fireworks, but also by the intensity of the explosions. The earth trembles, windows are smashed, and the more extensive the area of action, the greater the joy of the crowd, as well as the glory in which the Saint ascends. In the capital a competition such as this must have carried on until well after midnight (there are villages where the cost of the fireworks is equal to the entire budget of the municipality).

At a quarter past ten, when Madame Fredez leaves him, the fireworks have already begun. Roussel has told her that he will take some Soneryl and she has already noted it. She does not know how much he will take. As soon as he is alone, he starts to gulp down pills, helping them down with copious amounts of Fuiggi water (he drank a great deal of this, recalls Orlando, and this water not only helped him to swallow the numerous tablets but also had a diuretic effect). "That evening," says Orlando, "he did not even have the strength to raise a glass": but he was clearly exaggerating his state of weakness since, when Madame Fredez went out, he lifted the glass several times and then even a mattress. This detail of the mattress which he took down from the bed and placed between the connecting door and the balcony reinforces our conviction that he *did not wish to die*. As Francois Caradec informs us, Roussel "was afraid of falling out of bed"; for that reason he laid the mattress on the floor. This fear of falling out of bed, which is experienced by all children when they leave their cradle or small cot with bars for a normal bed (and those with disturbed sleep do, in fact, sometimes fall, with somewhat traumatic consequences of 'regression'), becomes, in adulthood, the symbol of another fear: that of falling into oblivion while asleep. If Roussel had decided to die, he would have lost this infantile fear of falling out of bed.

But it is more worthwhile to adhere to the facts mentioned in the judiciary archives and to Orlando's recollections. These are quite precise recollections, confirmed by the archives: and with time they have come to hang together like the plot of a detective novel. There are certain curious details, certain incoherences and contradictions. For example the one made by Madame Fredez when she states "I was told Monsieur Roussel was lying unconscious" and then corrects herself saying "I entered the room at the same time as the floor-porter." That morning Orlando caught her out: this aroused his suspicion and mistrust. "At about ten o'clock," recalls Orlando, "Kreuz came to tell me that Monsieur Roussel had not yet woken up. I went with him to the door of number 224—silence. We approached room number 226: we heard the water running in the bath. The lady was getting ready to take a bath and, consequently, we did not disturb her. Later, Kreuz came back to the door of number 224; he decided to go in. At precisely that moment the lady left her room." It was about eleven o'clock. Why did she take so long that morning? Why did she not worry first of all about Roussel's silence when Kreuz and Orlando had already been worrying about it for an hour?

There can only be one answer: Madame Fredez already knew that Roussel was dead. In her state of apprehension, at some time during the night or the morning—at any rate when the corridor was empty—she certainly entered room 224 (we must not forget that Roussel closed the connecting door but left the door on to the corridor open), discovering her friend dead and filled with distress and fear for the consequences which this death might have for her in a foreign country, she decided not to reveal anything and to wait for others to make the discovery.

If the police had been aware of the past life of Madame Fredez, a 'demi-mondiane' whom Roussel had chosen to be his companion and to whom he left a life annuity in his will, the inquest might have taken another direction. Charlotte Fredez was, therefore, feeling rather afraid but, except for the small contradiction quoted, she clearly behaved in such a way as to shorten the length of the enquiry. On the following day, the 15th. July, The Pact of Four was to be signed at the Palazzo Venezia; France was still "the latin sister": and probably Madame Fredez requested the immediate intervention of Monsieur Victor Clement the French Consul in Palermo. For her part the lady had the skill to inform those conducting the enquiry of the social position and the fame which Roussel enjoyed in France, even exaggerating it, and immediately to submit the page on which she had noted the different types of barbiturates and the doses which he took. The suspicion that the diary might have been written subsequently did not occur either to the police or the Magistrate, even though this was the time for suspicions. Apart from Madame Fredez's account of the social position and the repute of the deceased, apart from the French Consul's intervention which certainly took place immediately, apart from the testimony given by Professor Lombardo and the hotel staff which, in the eyes of the police and the Judge, was supplanted by the orgy of bottles and small tubes found in the room; apart from all these elements, there is no doubt that the Fascist rule, scrupulously observed by the police and the Magistrate, of keeping silence about all those cases in which the 'taedium vitae' brings about tragic conclusions, played a part in speeding up the course of the inquest. Even if not from a precise intention of will, the death of Roussel was effectively a suicide: and a stranger who came to put an end to his life in Italy when the glory of Fascist Italy was vibrant in the Atlantic skies and was sealing European peace with the pact of the four Great Powers, did not this death, besides alluding to the impossibility of living together, also allude to the impossibility of living in Fascist Italy? The Italian police were then extraordinarily sensitive about picking up allusions, to deciphering symbols and allegories. And is not suicide the very gesture which alludes most forcibly to the impossibility of living under tyranny? [13]

The Roussel case was therefore closed with an impressive speed by that very same police force, by that very same Magistrature whose functioning is generally of an impressive slowness and is atrociously burdensome for those who happen to find themselves caught up in it. All the 'acts' are dated the 14th, which means that everything took place in a little more than half a day. And no autopsy.

The Magistrate stopped for a moment over Madame Fredez's contradiction. He once more questioned the floor-porter Kreuz who declared: "This morning, at about ten o'clock, I was the first to enter Monsieur Roussel's room. To be more precise, Madame Fredez entered almost at the same time as myself. The door onto the corridor was open, with the key in the lock on the corridor side; even in the past Monsieur Roussel used to leave the door onto the corridor open, perhaps so as not to have to trouble himself each time he called the staff. The connecting door between Monsieur Roussel's room and that of Madame Fredez was closed with the key left in the lock on the inside of Roussel's room. Monsieur Roussel was lying unconscious on his back, in his underpants and shirt, on a mattress laid on the floor, with the top end towards the closed door to Madame Fredez's room. Nothing in the room had been moved."

One more testimony, that of the chambermaid Dora Chierici, thirty-eight years old, from Sarteano: "About one month ago, I was called by the bell to room 224, occupied by Monsieur Roussel. I found him unconscious on the floor beside his bed. I informed the Manager." The Magistrate asks one last question to confirm that Madame Fredez was not involved. The chambermaid replies: "Madame Fredez was then absent from Palermo" (she had left the day before). The inquest is over; the Magistrate, Margiotta, submits the 'acts' to the *illustrissimo signor procuratore del Re'* "for the provisions of the law". The Procurator returns them to him "so that he can deliver the order for burial, since it is not necessary to proceed to an autopsy". We wonder at what time, on the 14th, the King's Procurator returned the 'acts' to the Magistrate? Certainly not during office hours; probably around midnight. Quite exceptional enthusiasm.

But the fact that Professor Lombardo had failed at the time to make a report about the lesions which Roussel inflicted upon himself did not escape the Procurator. Consequently, while he was closing the Roussel case, he asked to be given the file "for eventual measures concerning Professor Lombardo".

Still on the 14th, the police sent a final report to the Superintendant and to the Magistrate, which is worth quoting here in its entirety: "At about 10 o'clock this morning, the French subject, Freder Carlotta, 53 years old, from Paris, daughter of the late Freder Carlo, staying in room number 226 of the Hôtel des Palmes, opened the door of room number 224 at the same time as the floor-porter of this same hotel, Kreur Antonio. The room was occupied by the Frenchman, ROUSSEL Raymond, lover of this woman, born in Paris on the 20-1-1887, resident in Paris, 20 rue Quenten Bauchant.[14] She found his body supine on a mattress placed on the floor. Once informed, the hotel manager, Serena Leopoldo, notified this office. The Commissioner of the State Police, Doctor Giuseppe La Farina, Brigadier Zingales Giuseppe and other police officers arrived on the scene, noted what we stated above and informed the Judiciary Authority. From the inquests and checks executed by this office it immediately transpired that Roussel's death was due to poisoning caused by the large quantity of narcotics which he had swallowed. In fact, in the medical report undertaken by Doctor Rabboni Federico, it was noted that death was due to poisoning. On the table two empty "Sonneril" tubes were found, each one containing 20 capsules which Roussel had certainly swallowed the previous evening. In the presence of the Magistrate, Doctor Margiotta, the body was examined and on it were found lesions caused by a blade instrument, among them a deeper one on the left wrist. When interrogated, the said Freder Carlotta, who had been living with Roussel for about 23 years, declared that he was a somewhat neurasthenic person, that his illness had become particularily bad these last two years, that was occupied by Roussel and the other by the said Freder; at night, the nothing but take narcotics which he said put him into a special state of drunkenness. The abovementioned, who had arrived at Palermo with his lover about forty days before, hoping for some improvement in his health because of the mild climate, had rented two connecting rooms in the hotel. One room was occupied by Roussel and the other by Madame Freder. At night, the abovementioned opened the connecting door and passed through to his mistress. For about 10 days, however, the connecting door had been locked on the inside by Roussel, who did not wish to be disturbed by Freder. However, he left the other door onto the outside corridor ajar, so as not to have to trouble himself to open it when the staff came. Freder added that on the 2nd. of this month her friend, his illness having worsened, had entered the bathroom which connected with his room and had tried to commit suicide using a Gilet razor. This explains the wounds found on him which we mentioned earlier. The said Freder had taken the razor away from him in time, afterwards taking care to remove all weapons from his sight. Professor Lombardo Michele, the hotel Doctor who was treating Roussel, affirmed that the abovementioned was suffering from neurasthenia, for which he was taking barbiteirute (sic) substances which produced in him a state of drunkenness and that several times the Doctor had had to call round urgently to stop blood-poisoning. He had also intervened on the day Roussel had attempted to commit suicide to dress his wounds. The corpse, as we said earlier, was lying supine in a shirt and underpants on a mattress taken from the bed and laid on the floor. His head was turned towards the connecting door leading to the room occupied by his mistress, which was locked on the inside. After the examination, Doctor Margiotta ordered the removal of the corpse and the closing of the room with seals placed on the door bearing the stamp of this police station, while the key of the other door onto the corridor was entrusted to the hotel Manager signor Sirena. The appropriation of the small bottles and the small tubes of narcotics, including the small empty ones, was ordered. The package containing the objects already quoted, as well as two private letters bearing no relation to the affair, was placed and duly sealed in a cardboard box, which I am having deposited at the Chancellery of this Royal Magistrature. As a complement to my internal telegram of this morning, I inform You that *in this affair any responsibility of a third party can be excluded."*

This letter is not only a good example of police prose, but also of the inattentiveness and carelessness which can be considered as typical of this profession which should not permit such inattentiveness and carelessness. Fredez becomes Freder; the Manager of the hotel is transformed into Sirena; and, most serious of all, Colonel Gillette, the inventor of the razor which bears his name, becomes Gilet. If a policeman cannot grasp the name and face of the Colonel and cannot perceive that he is naming an object and not an inventor, how can he be expected to see those remains on the scene of a crime which provide clues? (Besides, the letter is carefully corrected by hand wherever the Vice-Superintendent who signed it found something to correct.) The grossly Gallic manner in which the relationship between Roussel and Fredez is spoken of is worth noting. The police would have been astonished to learn that the abovementioned did not pass through to his mistress at night and that, moreover, Fredez had never actually been the mistress of Raymond Roussel.

Another thing to note is the Italianisation of the proper names. The war against the linguistic "barbarian domination" which France and England exercised over the Italians had already begun: consequently, the functionaries, even if they wrote in rather doubtful Italian, enthusiastically set about translating Charlotte into Carlotta and Charles into Carlo.[15]

On the 21st. July, at the request of the French Consul, "in accordance with Article 9, paragraph 2 of the Franco-Italian Consular Convention of the 26th. July 1862," the seals placed on room number 224 of the Hôtel des

Palmes on the 14th. were removed. The Magistrate handed over all the "personal effects" of the deceased, Raymond Roussel, to Monsieur Victor Clement and Monsieur Clement received them "in the interests of the possible heirs". A double record of this handing over was written out in Italian and French.

The 'acts' thus completed were once again handed over to the King's Procurator, Stefano Mercadante, who initiated (and then immediately closed) proceedings with regard to Professor Lombardo.

On the 6th. August, Professor Lombardo 'appeared' before the Procurator and declared: "I did not mention the lesions which Roussel had inflicted upon himself with a 'gillette' blade some days before, both because they were light wounds which would certainly have healed in four or five days in the case of a normal person not affected by chronic poisoning, and because—and this is the real reason—I was absolutely certain that these lesions were not due to a crime. Indeed, I knew the subject's state of health and, on this occasion, I was able to learn the truth about what had happened from Roussel himself and from what the latter's companion and the hotel staff told me. Having been able to ascertain that there was no question of a crime, I considered it unnecessary to present a certificate." The Procurator, convinced that Professor Lombardo had acted "without wilful misrepresentation", that very day ordered the transfer of the 'acts' to the archives where we found them thirty-seven years later.

Michel Ney, Duc d'Elchingen, interviewed by Jean Chatard and Robert Momeux (*Bizarre*, 34/35, 1964) on whether "it can be affirmed, written, that it is a question of suicide," replies: "Listen! . . . Personally I did not see him because I was not there, but they wrote to me from down there . . . Palermo Town Hall. They even gave me particulars he cut his wrists in the bath . . . I am almost certain it was suicide. And I will tell you why . . . In his will . . . He had no more money; he apologised to me saying: 'Listen, I'm really sorry, but I haven't left you anything . . . that has been one of my great faults and I apologise for it . . .' Consequently, he knew very well he was going to die . . ."

In the 'acts relative', as we have seen, the word 'suicide' never occurs. How could Palermo Town Hall give 'particulars' to the Duc d'Elchingen when it only received notification of death without the cause even being mentioned as is the usual procedure? Neither is it conceivable that the Magistrate investigating might have written to the Duke. Only the French Consul would have been able to send him information; but not erroneous information, because the Duke seems certain that his uncle committed suicide—by cutting his wrists in the bathroom and not by a heavy dose of barbiturates. And then he knows nothing about the woman who accompanied Roussel; he even doubts that Roussel went to Palermo in the company of a woman. But let us now transcribe that part of the interview which follows the affirmation that Roussel committed suicide by cutting his wrists, because he had no more money:

"*Jean Chatard:* His goodness, in that sentence in his will . . .

Michel Ney: Ah! his goodness always comes back to me . . . and the proof is that now I'm profiting from it . . . He was really sorry not to leave me anything . . .

Jean Chatard: The explanation about the door which connected his housekeeper's room and which was bolted for the first time, in the Palermo hotel . . .[16] according to you, these facts are erroneous?

Michel Ney: Listen, his housekeeper was a nurse who was perhaps with him at that time . . .

Jean Chatard: His housekeeper has been spoken of . . .

Michel Ney: Perhaps she was someone he had had go out there? But I can guarantee he did not leave with a housekeeper.

Jean Chatard: You saw him leave alone?

Michel Ney: Yes. He had hired a car and a chauffeur . . . moreover on his return the chauffeur tried to blackmail me . . . So there couldn't have been a housekeeper during this journey."

One begins to suspect that the Duke's information concerning the death of his uncle, had been received solely from the chauffeur; the latter, hurrying back from Palermo, presented himself at his house to blackmail him with the tale of a special relationship with Roussel. Naturally, it was not in the chauffeur's interests to speak of Madame Fredez whose presence, at a time when certain things caused more scandal than they do today, made the special relationship improbable and did not accord with the way of life, completely decent, so respectful of appearances, of a man like Roussel. Neither did it suit the chauffeur to relate how Roussel had really died; knowing that he was arriving in advance of a possible official communication from the French Consul or the Italian Authorities, he gave an account of the death which left the nephew in absolutely no doubt that it was suicide. Or perhaps the chauffeur really was convinced that Roussel had died by cutting his wrists; that Roussel had repeated, with a fatal outcome, what had been no more than attempted suicide ten days before. Because—Gaetano Orlando remembers clearly, and the fact strengthens certain of his suspicions about Roussel's death—on the

14th. July the chauffeur had disappeared. As we said before, he was not staying at the same hotel. So someone informed him that Roussel was dead, that he had committed suicide; and that was enough to make him return to Paris. Strangely, during the course of the inquest nobody mentioned him; neither Madame Fredez nor the hotel staff. If someone had mentioned him (even in passing, as Orlando does today when recalling the evening of the 13th.: "we carried him, the chauffeur and I, from the car to the lift and from the lift to his room"), the police would not have failed to look for him and, when they could not find him, to intensify their search. Even if accidental death or suicide was taken to be certain, no police force in the world would have foregone hearing such an important witness—and such a suspicious one, from the moment he had slipped away, presumably to avoid testifying. The fact that the hotel staff did not mention him is comprehensible: the habit of discretion, and then in a town like Palermo. But how is it that Madame Fredez did not seek out her compatriot at such a difficult, anxious moment; how is it that she did not mention him in her statements to the police and to the Magistrate?[17]

Undeniably there are many obscure points concerning the last days and the death of Raymond Roussel; and so, if considered from a suspicious point of view, the events take on something of the mysterious—like a *detective story*.

Let us try to sum up and to put in order these obscure points: 1. Roussel leaves Paris in a state of health which is not ruinous. He faces the journey by car, renouncing his comfortable 'roulotte'. The nephew, who sees him leave, is not alarmed (and when some years later Chatard says; "He was very ill when he arrived in Palermo", Michel Ney answers abstractedly: "His nerves, perhaps, yes . . ."). 2. In Palermo Roussel is very ill; physically and mentally his condition worsens. Despite the continued deterioration of his health, he decides on a long stay in the town, from the fact that she returned to Paris to collect the money that they would need, it does not appear that Madame Fredez was opposed to this stay. The idea that she and Roussel decided on "a long stay" in Palermo because of the "mild climate", would not seem bizarre in January, but in mid-July . . ! 3. The day following Madame Fredez' departure, Roussel collapses; he is looked after and makes a good recovery according to the hotel Manager, a complete recovery according to Professor Lombardo. But his condition gets worse on the lady's return. 4. On the evening of the 13th. Roussel is totally exhausted; he cannot stay upright. He did not have—according to Orlando—the strength to lift a glass. But, once he is alone, he shifts an enormous armchair, takes the mattress down from the bed, places it between the connecting door and the balcony and places two cushions on it in a bizarre manner—so as to position himself between the two and not to rest his head on them. 5. On the next day, the 14th., until 10 o'clock, Madame Fredez shows no alarm over Roussel's silence; she leaves her room when she hears that the floor-porter, Kreuz, is about to enter the adjoining room. 6. In the room, not one paper written by Roussel is found; On the other hand, a note of the daily doses of barbiturates which he took and their effects written by Madame Fredez is found. 7. On the morning of the 24th., the chauffeur does not turn up; he disappears from Palermo. This does not appear to surprise Madame Fredez; she avoids making any reference about the *disparu* (missing) chauffeur to the investigating officers. 8. Upon her return to Paris, Madame Fredez does not go to see Michel Ney; she makes no attempt to meet him. She was, however, aware of Roussel's affection for his nephew and that his nephew was his heir. If she had visited the Duke, the chauffeur would not *"faire de chantage"* (be able to blackmail him). If the Duke submitted to blackmail he did so because he did not know that his uncle was with Fredez at the Hôtel des Palmes and that the chauffeur was staying at a-nother hotel. Even if all three of them had been in the same hotel, knowing the propriety of Roussel, his delicacy and his concern not to reveal anything about himself, he would never have believed in a 'ménage à trois'. Besides if there was a special relationship with the chauffeur, the staff of the Palmes never had the least suspicion of it. (Orlando remembers the young chauffeur very well and the latter had told him how, as a taxi-driver, he had one day picked up Roussel, who had immediately engaged him for the journey to Italy.) Furthermore, when the Rousselian cult depicted Fredez as the faithful, devoted companion of the genius, as well as the witness of his last days and his death, it seems that she spoke of his suicide by cutting his wrists. Had she forgotten how things had actually happened, or was she simply lying (through interest)? In either case, there is a mystery.

But perhaps these obscure points which emerge from the papers and recollections appeared quite probable and explicable at the time. The facts of life always become more complex and obscure, more ambiguous and equi-vocal than they really are, once they are written down—that is, when, from 'acts relative' they become, so to speak, 'acts absolute'. As that policeman in Graham Greene said: "We can hang more people than the newspapers can write about." So can we, after all.

—1971

Raymond Roussel's place of death.

Notes

1. See note no. 8 to the previous essay for the meanings of 'Acts'.
2. The exact name is *Grand hotel et des Palmes*. The history of this hotel, from Wagner's stay to the American occupation and to the vicissitudes of the regional government, particularily during the 'Milazzo' period, might be written as a chapter of Sicily's splendour and wretchedness from the Savoie to the Republic. [Author's note]
3. Roussel's father was called Eugene, his mother Marguerite Moreau-Chaslon. [Author's note]
4. Probably after the gap, beginning at the conclusion of the first chapter: "Now, examination proved that this was the very niche . . . " Or from page 35, where the second chapter begins? [Author's note]
5. Third edition of *Impressions*, tenth of *Locus Solus*. We do not know much about this, but we doubt that so many editions existed, except in Roussel's mythomaniac imagination. [Author's note] Recent research seems to confirm Sciascia's supposition.
6. Orlando, now retired, works at the Hôtel des Palmes on days when official banquets or wedding receptions are held. His memory of the Roussel affair remains clear; he even remembers on which days of the week certain things happened. (One detail which struck him, and of which there is no mention in the reports, is that Roussel had had an ejaculation that night, probably as he was dying. Orlando still speaks of it with a great deal of disgust, amazement and unease. Why was this detail suppressed in the medical report, when judiciary reports usually abound in the crudest of details.) On the other hand, Bertolino the barber, who is still working, retains only a vague recollection. He saw Roussel twice to cut his hair (he used to trim his own beard). [Author's note]
7. 25,000 francs was equivalent to 19,275 lire at that time. An Italian family from the clerical class, the back-bone of Fascism, lived on an average of 600 lire per month. [Author's note]
8. Francois Caradec informs us that Dufrène (Fredez = Dez-fré = Dufrène) was, as she herself told Michel Leiris, a pseudonym which she had chosen "to carry out her occupation as a kept woman, because she came from a bourgeois family and had been brought up in a convent". [Author's note]
9. The successors of the notary, Constantin, had their office, in 1964, at 15, rue Rodier (c.f. *Bizarre* 34/35). [Author's note]
10. Sleeping tablets and barbiturates act on certain individuals to produce firstly a fairly long period of sleep and then a fairly lucid state of euphoria. From the first effect, therefore, a second effect emerges, and we are given to understand, in the *Manual of Pharmacology* by Kuschinsky and Lullmann, that with such individuals, in habitual usage and addiction, the heavy dose is reduced to a small dose through sleep, and that this small dose can produce a state of excitement: "a small dose of any narcotic is capable of producing a state of excitement". But the margin of effectiveness of the small dose is only maintained through the progressive increasing of the original dose which is eliminated through sleep. [Author's note]
11. But he did not wish to die and he immediately called for help. "I was the first to come along: I helped him to get up. Monsieur Roussel laughed and said: 'Orlando, Orlando' . . ." Orlando confirms this statement which he made to Mauro De Mauro on the 10th. December 1964 (*L'ora* newspaper). [Author's note]
12. Professor Lombardo recalls that, some days before, Roussel, leaning out of the window, had thrown money to the passers-by. [Author's note]
13. On the 15th. July, neither of the two Palermo newspapers—the morning paper *Il*

Giornale di Sicilia, and the evening paper *L'ora*—mention Roussel's death. The pages of the town chronicle record the discovery of human skeletons in the Piazza Acquasanta, the kicking of a peasant by a mule, an assurance agent beaten in via Cavour and "the unhappiness of a barber in his second marriage". Not a single word about the fact that, as in Pirandello's short novel, "a certain man has died at the hotel". [Author's note]

14. 20 rue Quenten Bauchant. The nephew will say: ". . . he was living in the same house as myself at the time . . . that is, my mother's house." [Author's note]

15. In the death certificate, the 'y' of Raymond becomes 'i' and his father, Eugène, becomes Eugenio. [Author's note]

16. We know that Roussel had closed the connecting door for several days. Chatard did not know this and thought that he had only closed it on the evening of the 13th., since he had decided to die and he did not want to upset Madame Fredez. Up to now, only very little was known about the death of Roussel. On the third of August 1933, in *Paris-Midi,* Pierre Lazareff spoke of the "edifying death in a Palermo convent of Raymond Roussel, the extremely wealthy, unusual dramatic author". Thirty years later, Michel Ney, Roussel's nephew, also possesses inaccurate information and vouches for its accuracy to Jean Chatard and Robert Momeux. [Author's note]

17. In the quoted article by Mauro De Mauro, Professor Lombardo says at one time that Roussel had got rid of the chauffeur, paying him and giving him the car. But the car did not belong to Roussel (he had hired it in Paris), and Orlando remembers clearly that the chauffeur was in Palermo on the evening of the 13th. Besides, the fact that he tried blackmail (or rather, succeeded in it), proves that he had left Palermo knowing that Roussel was dead. It is true that he could have learnt about it from the newspapers. But the papers which mentioned it (few, we think), were late in receiving the news, while we are given to understand that the chauffeur introduced himself to Michel Ney immediately after his return from Palermo. [Author's note]

I. M. Raymond Roussel's House on Wheels
II. Raymond Roussel in English — Bibliography

1. The motorised "roulotte" (gypsy caravan) photographed at
M. Raymond Roussel's property in Neuilly.

F.T.
M. Raymond Roussel's House on Wheels
— Full-scale Motorised Camping —

Translation   Antony Melville

We do not pretend to preach to the readers of the *Revue du Touring Club de France* the joys that camping offers to its enthusiasts.

Indeed in almost every issue we have a camper promoting the delights of driving off along the roads freely and heartily and stopping at will beside a stream, or in a field, a meadow, a wood—sleeping beneath the open sky with but a slender roof over his head, far removed from the rest of mankind asleep inside their houses.

We propose here to describe an extremely ingenious, very comfortable means of 'full-scale' camping.

M. Baudry de Saunier in his book "The Joy of Camping" divided camping enthusiasts into two tribes, who show a certain amount of rivalry between them, but get along all the same because they fly the same flag: the *Spartans* and the *Sybarites*.

The Spartans are the ones that go about either on foot or by bicycle carrying their house (a canvas house which weighs no more than 20 lbs. when fully furnished) upon their backs. They are the valiant troopers of camping.

The Sybarites, on the other hand, are the ones that have their houses carried upon a motor vehicle. And of course they want that house to be as comfortable as possible. They mean to recreate in the middle of the woods, or the middle of the fields, the comforts and pleasures of their own home.

So it is with the Sybarites in mind that we describe the very luxurious and practical house on wheels devised by M. Raymond Roussel. The author of *Impressions d'Afrique*, which is aclaimed by distinguished minds as a work of genius, has had built from his plans an automobile 30 feet long by 8 feet wide.

The car is really a small house. In fact it comprises, by means of an ingenious system: a sitting-room (figure 2), a bedroom (figure 3), a study (figure 4), a bathroom (figure 6) and even a small dormitory for the staff of three man-servants (two chauffeurs and a valet).

The bodywork built by Lacoste is very elegant, and the interior both original and ingenious. To take two examples: the Bedroom can in the

2.

3.

4.

2. The sitting-room/bedroom arranged as a sitting-room, with mirrors, lit by generous windows and provided with comfortable arm-chairs. 3. The sitting-room/bedroom set up for the night. The bed, which during the day is hidden in the panelling, swings out. 4. Another disposition of the sitting-room/bedroom: the study.

daytime be turned either into a study or a sitting-room, while the forward part (behind the driver's seat) at night turns into a little bedroom where the three man-servants can rest and wash (there is a basin in the panelling—to be seen to the left of the driver's seat (figure 5).

The interior of M. Raymond Roussel's house on wheels comes from Maples.

There is electric heating and a paraffin stove. The hot water for the bath also runs on Paraffin.

The furniture is designed to cater for every need. There is even a Fichet safe.

An excellent wireless set can pick up any European station.

This brief description gives some idea of how this remarkable villa on wheels—to which can be added a towable kitchen—affords its owner all the comforts of his own home on a scarcely reduced scale.

The chassis on which this luxurious installation is constructed is a Saurer chassis. On the flat its cruising speed is 25 m.p.h. It can negotiate steep hills without fear thanks to an engine-braking system.

It has a very 'tight' turning circle, which is very useful for twisting mountain roads.

M. Raymond Roussel did not design and build his caravan—as he modestly refers to it—as a mere whim, without intending to use it.

As soon as it was built the caravan set off last year for a round trip of 2000 miles through Switzerland and Alsace. Every evening M. Roussel had a different view.

He returned from his trip with incomparable impressions.[1]

This year, at the start of Summer, he took to the road to follow his wandering fancy, in search of constantly changing sensations.

This version of full-scale motorised camping is of course not within everyone's means.[2] It is all the same surprising that it should be so completely unknown to those who could actually put it into practise.

It is to be hoped that the example of M. Raymond Roussel will be understood and followed by numerous sybarites and that the day will come when many houses on wheels will run on the world's roads, to the subtle satisfaction of their occupants.

Notes

1. ! [Trans.]
2. Either as a motorised "Roulotte" or as a touring caravan attached to a motor-car [Author's note]

5.

6.

5. The "staff quarters" by day; at night three folding couchettes turn it into a dormitory. 6. The bathroom, an excellent combination of hygene and minimal surface area, that is to say, marrying luxury and simplicity.

RAYMOND ROUSSEL IN ENGLISH
Compiled by Alastair Brotchie

There are various bibliographies of Raymond Roussel, the most comprehensive, in French and in Italian, are to be found in *Melusine, VI, 'Raymond Roussel en Gloire,'* Editions L'Age d'Homme, Lausanne, 1984; and in German, in *Raymond Roussel: Eine Dokumentation,* edition text + kritik, Munich, 1977. The best in English is this one! It owes a great deal to the bibliography in Trevor Winkfield's translation of 'How I Wrote Certain of my Books' (Va. below) and to an unpublished checklist assembled by Alec Gordon.

The contents of the present volume are listed here for completeness sake, they are indicated by: Atlas Anth. 4.

TRANSLATIONS OF WORKS BY ROUSSEL

Complete translations are indicated by a *, and are listed first, extracts follow in chronological order.

I. *Impressions d'Afrique,* Lemerre, 1910.

    a. Impressions of Africa*, trans. L. Foord & Rayner Heppenstall, Calder & Boyars, London, and University of California Press, Berkeley, 1967. Reprinted John Calder, 1983.

    b. Extract trans. Marie Jolas, *Transition,* 12, 1928.

    c. Extracts trans. Edouard Roditi, *View,* Series III, 4, 1943 & Series IV, 1, 1944; reprinted *A Night with Jupiter,* Dobson, N.Y., 1947.

    d. Extract (ch. 1), trans. John Ashbery, *Portfolio and ARTnews Annual,* 6, Autumn 1962.

    e. Extract ('The Poet and the Morisco'), trans. Rayner Heppenstall, *New Directions,* 18, 1964.

    f. Extracts trans. Marcel Jean, *The Autobiography of Surrealism,* Viking Press, N.Y., 1980.

II. *Locus Solus,* Lemerre, 1914.

    a. Locus Solus*, trans. R. C. Cunningham, Calder & Boyars, London & University of California Press, Berkeley, 1970. Reprinted John Calder 1983

    b. Extract trans. Harry Mathews, *Locus Solus,* V, 1962.

    c. Extracts trans. Marcel Jean, *The Autobiography of Surrealism,* Viking Press, N.Y., 1980.

III. *L'Étoile au Front,* Lemerre, 1925.

    a. Extract ('The Terrace'), part of Act I, sc. 3, trans. Rayner Heppenstall, *New Directions,* 18, 1964.

    b. Extract, Act I, scs. 1 & 2, trans. Paul Hammond, *Juillard,* 8, Winter 1970-1.

    c. Extract ('Two Narratives from "The Star on the Forehead" '), part of Act

II, sc. 4, trans. John Harman, *Atlas Anthology,* 3, 1985.

IV. *Nouvelles Impressions d'Afrique,* Lemerre, 1932.

    a. Extract (Canto 3), trans. Kenneth Koch, *Art & Literature,* 2, Summer 1964, reprinted in Va.

V. *Comment j'ai écrit certains de mes livres,* Lemerre, 1935.

This book comprises the title essay, stories and texts by Roussel, and texts by Janet and Tartakower.

Title Essay.

    a. How I wrote Certain of my Books, trans. Trevor Winkfield, Sun, N.Y., 1975 & 1977. Includes the title essay, plus '(A)N(ECD)OTES' by Trevor Winkfield and reprints of IVa. and Ashbery a and c.

    b. Extracts trans. Marcel Jean, *The Autobiography of Surrealism,* Viking Press, N.Y., 1980.

Stories by Roussel.

    c.? Two stories trans. Lindy Heppenstall, *Harper's Bazaar,* Dec. 1963. (R. Heppenstall refers to these translations in *New Directions* 18, however they do not appear in the British edition of the magazine.)

    d. The Greenish Skin, trans. Rayner Heppenstall, *New Directions,* 18, 1964; reprinted in Heppenstall b.

    e. Among the Blacks, trans. R. Padgett, *Bones,* 2, N.Y., 1968.

    f. The Old Gentleman's White Curls, and The Skate's Scales (two stories), trans. Rayner Heppenstall, *London Magazine,* Vol. 8, 5, August 1968.

    g. The Stopping-Place, trans. Trevor Winkfield, *Juillard,* 7, Winter 1968-9.

    h. Among the Blacks, trans. R. Padgett & Trevor Winkfield, *Juillard,* 8, Winter 1970-1.

    i. Among the Blacks, trans. Alastair Brotchie & Cecilia Muir, *Art Exchange Anthology,* 1973.

    j. Second Document to Serve as an Outline, trans. Joe Hedges, *Atlas Anthology,* 1, 1983.

Texts by Janet & Tartakower.

    k. The Psychological Characteristics of Ecstacy, by Pierre Janet, trans. Claire Jakens, *Atlas Anthology,* 2, 1984.

    l. The Psychological Characteristics of Ecstasy, by Pierre Janet, trans. John Harman, Atlas Anth. 4.

VI. Other works by Roussel.

    a. Correspondence with Charlotte Dufrene, trans. Paul Hammond, *Juillard,* Winter 1970-1.

    b. 59 Instructions for Drawings, trans. and introduced by Trevor Winkfield, *Sun,* vol. 4, 2, Spring 1975.

    c. In Havana, trans John Ashbery, Atlas Anth. 4.

VII. CRITICAL WORKS IN ENGLISH

Book length studies indicated by *.

John ASHBERY

    a. Re-establishing Raymond Roussel, *Portfolio and ARTnews Annual*, 6, Autumn 1962; reprinted in Va. as 'On Raymond Roussel', and under the same title, with a short postscript in Foucault a.

    b. Introduction to Raymond Roussel's "In Havana" [Un Inedit de Raymond Roussel, *L'Arc*, 19, Winter 1962], trans. John Ashbery, Atlas Anth. 4.

    c. In Darkest Language, *New York Times Book Review*, Oct. 29, 1967; reprinted in Va.

André BRETON

    a. Raymond Roussel [Raymond Roussel, *le Minotaure*, 10, 1937; *Anthologie de l'Humour Noir*, ed. du Sagittaire, 1940], trans. Martin Sorrell, Atlas Anth. 4.

Michel BUTOR

    a. The Methods of Raymond Roussel [Sur les procedes de Raymond Roussel, *Repertoire 1*, Minuit, 1960, periodical publication (?) 1950], trans. Roderick Masterton, Atlas Anth. 4.

Roger CARDINAL

    a. Enigma, *Twentieth Century Studies*, 12, 1974.

Michel CARROUGES

    a. Directions for Use / What is a Batchelor Machine?, [*Le Macchine Celibi/ The Batchelor Machines*, Alfieri, Venice, 1975.

Ross CHAMBERS

    a. Literature as Parenthesis: Raymond Roussel, *Meanjin Quaterly*, 29, March 1970.

A. CHERNIACK-TZURIEL

    a. Roussel's "Impressions of Africa", *The Drama Review*, June 1976.

Jean COCTEAU

    a. Opium [*Opium. Journal d'une desintoxication*, Stock, 1930], trans. E. Boyd, Longmans, 1932 & G. Allen and Unwin 1933; trans. M. Crosland and S. Road, Peter Owen, 1957 & Icon books 1961.

Julio CORTAZAR

    a. Of Another Batchelor Machine [first publication details not available] in *Around the Day in Eighty Worlds*, trans. Thomas Christensen, North Point Press, San Francisco, 1986.

Salvador DALI

    a. Raymond Roussel, "Nouvelles Impressions d'Afrique" [*le Surréalisme A.S.D.L.R.*, 6, 1933], trans. Martin Sorrell, Atlas Anth. 4.

Jean FERRY

    a. Raymond Roussel in Paradise [Raymond Roussel au paradis, *Le Mecanicien et autres contes*, Gallimard 1953], trans. Paul Hammond, *Juillard*, 3, Winter 1968-9; reprinted Atlas Anth. 4.

    b. Two letters to Jacques Brunius, trans. Antony Melville, Atlas Anth. 4.

Michel FOUCAULT

    a. *Death and the Labyrinth. The World of Raymond Roussel [Raymond Roussel, Gallimard, 1963], trans. Charles Ruas, Doubleday, N.Y. 1986, Athlone Press, London, 1987.

Rayner HEPPENSTALL

    a. Raymond Roussel. A Preliminary Study. *New Directions*, 18, 1964.

b. *Raymond Roussel. A Critical Study. Calder & Boyars, 1967.

Leslie HILL
a. Raymond Roussel and the Place of Literature, *Modern Language Review*, 74, 4, 1979.

Pierre JANET
a. The Psychological Characteristics of Ecstasy [from *De l'angoisse à l'extase*, Alcan, 1926] see Vk. & l.

Martin JAY
a. In the Empire of the Gaze: Foucault and the denigration of Vision in Twentieth-century French Thought, in *Foucault. A Critical Reader*, ed. D. C. Hoy, Blackwell, Oxford, 1986.

Gilbert LASCAULT
a. Mechanisms/The Fuck/ The Non-Fuck/ Painting/ Play on Words/Etc..., *Le Macchine Celibi/The Batchelor Machines*, Alfieri, Venice, 1975.

Michel LEIRIS
a. Conception and Reality in the Work of Raymond Roussel [Conception et Realite chez Raymond Roussel, *Critique*, 89, 1954; reprinted *Epaves*, Pauvert, 1973], trans. John Ashbery, *Art & Literature*, 2, 1964; reprinted Atlas Anth. 4.

Carl LOVITT
a. Locus Solus: Literary Solitaire, *Sub-stance*, 10, 1974.

Harry MATHEWS
a. Roussel and Venice [Roussel et Venise, *L'Arc*, 68, 1977], co-written with Georges Perec, trans. Antony Melville & Harry Mathews, *Atlas Anthology 3*, 1985.

J. H. MATTHEWS
a. Beyond Realism: Raymond Roussel's Machines, *Fiction, Form and Experience*, ed. K. E. Grant. France-Quebec, Montreal, 1976.
b. Raymond Roussel's *Impressions d'Afrique*, ch. in *Surrealism & the Novel*, Ann Arbor: The University of Michigan Press, 1976.

Robert de MONTESQUIOU
a. A Difficult Author [from *Elus et Appeles*, Emil-Paul freres, 1921], extract trans. Catherine Allan, Atlas Anth. 4.

Georges PEREC
a. See Mathews a. above.

David PIERSSENS
a. The Power of Babel [*La Tour de Babil*, Minuit, 1976], trans. Carl Lovitt, Routledge Kegan Paul, 1980.

J. P. PLOTTEL
a. Roussel's Mechanisms of Language, *Dada/Surrealism*, 5, 1976.
b. Structures and Counterstructures in Roussel's *Impressions d'Afrique*, *Dada/Surrealism*, 5, 1975.

David PORUSH
a. Roussel's Device for the Perfection of Fiction, ch. 2 of *The Soft Machine*, Methuen, 1985.

Rene RADRIZZANI
a. Roussel, Discoverer of New Worlds, *Le Macchine Celibi/The Batchelor Machines*, Alfieri, Venice, 1975.

Jean RICARDOU
a. Elocutory Disappearance [Disparition elocutoire, *Actes relatifs a la mort de Raymond Roussel*, L'Herne, 1972], trans. Alec Gordon, Atlas Anth 4.

Alain ROBBE-GRILLET
- a. Riddles and Transparencies in the Work of Raymond Roussel [Enigme et Transparence chez Raymond Roussel, *Pour un nouveau roman*, Minuit, 1963], trans. Barbara Wright, *Snapshots & Towards a New Novel*, Calder & Boyars, 1965; reprinted Atlas Anth. 4.

Leon ROUDIEZ
- a. French Fiction Today: A New Direction, ch. 1 "Raymond Roussel", Rutgers University Press, 1972.

Leonardo SCIASCIA
- a. Acts Relative to the Death of Raymond Roussel [*Atti relativi alla morte di Raymond Roussel*, Sellerio, Palermo, 1972] trans. Alec Gordon, Atlas Anth. 4.

Philippe SOUPAULT
- a. Raymond Roussel [Raymond Roussel, *Littérature*, April, 1922] trans. Antony Melville, Atlas Anth. 4.

Allan STOEKL
- a. Politics, Writing, Mutilation. The Cases of Bataille, Blanchot, Roussel, Leiris and Ponge. University of Minnesota Press, 1986. Ch. 3: "Roussel's Revivifications of History".

Roger VITRAC
- a. Raymond Roussel [Raymond Roussel, *Nouvelle Revue Francaise*, February, 1928], partial trans. Kathleen Cannell, *Transition*, 12, 1928; complete trans. K. Cannell & Antony Melville, Atlas Anth. 4.

Trevor WINKFIELD
- a. (A)N(ECD)OTES, see Va.

ADDENDA

F.T.
- a. M. Raymond Roussel's House on Wheels. [La maison roulante de M. Raymond Roussel, *La Revue de Touring-Club de France*, August, 1926] Trans. A. Melville, Atlas Anth. 4.

EVENTUALLY

(for it is impossible to overestimate the difficulties of translation)

ATLAS PRESS

will be publishing

NEW IMPRESSIONS OF AFRICA

by

RAYMOND ROUSSEL

Translated by Stanley CHAPMAN

Introduced by John ASHBERY

Illustrated by ZO

The edition will be limited to 500 copies, casebound, and will accord with Roussel's design of the French first edition—all the illustrations will appear within uncut pages, the text will appear on every fourth page. In addition the French text will be reproduced and we will include Roussel's instructions for each picture to Zo, who, commisioned through a detective agency, was not allowed to read the text he was illustrating!

You may reserve a copy of this edition by writing to us.

Approximate price £12.

FORTHCOMING IN 1987 & 1988

THE SKIN OF DREAMS by RAYMOND QUENEAU
Translated by H. J. Kaplan.
MY FRIEND PIERROT by RAYMOND QUENEAU
Translated by Barbara Wright.
Two of Queneau's best novels both in superb translations. No further recommendation required!

THE TABLETS by ARMAND SCHWERNER
Schwerner's "Tablets", fictional poems in the form of Sumero-Akkadian tablets have been in progress since the late sixties. The result is a tour-de-force on every level.

THE BENJAMIN PERET ANTHOLOGY
THE major selection from Péret's works, a large volume containing his novel 'Mort aux Vaches', stories, poems, political texts, art criticism, polemics. With a major biographical essay by Rachel Stella based on hitherto undiscovered information about his political activities. Photographs, bibliography, in short —the business.

We have other plans, including a major work by ANDRE BRETON, for information and up-dates, write to be put on our mailing list:

ATLAS PRESS, 10, PARK STREET, THE BOROUGH, LONDON SE1 9AB

Obscurum per obscurius, ignotum per ignotius.